KT-227-429

# COPYRIGHT

## interpreting the law for libraries, archives and information services

Fourth edition

# Graham P. Cornish

facet publishing

© Graham P. Cornish 1990, 1997, 1999, 2001, 2004

Published by
Facet Publishing
7 Ridgmount Street
London WC1E 7AE

Facet Publishing is wholly owned by CILIP: the Chartered Institute of Library and Information Professionals.

Graham P. Cornish has asserted his right under the Copyright, Designs and Patents Act, 1988, to be identified as the author of this work.

Except as otherwise permitted under the Copyright, Designs and Patents Act, 1988, this publication may only be reproduced, stored or transmitted in any form or by any means, with the prior permission of the publisher, or, in the case of reprographic reproduction, in accordance with the terms of a licence issued by The Copyright Licensing Agency. Enquiries concerning reproduction outside those terms should be sent to Facet Publishing, 7 Ridgmount Street, London WC1E 7AE.

First published 1990
Second edition 1997
Third edition 1999
Third revised edition 2001
This fourth edition 2004

British Library Cataloguing in Publication Data
A catalogue record for this book is available from the British Library.

ISBN 1-85604-508-0

Typeset in Humanist 521 and Garamond by Facet Publishing.
Printed and made in Great Britain by MPG Books Ltd, Bodmin, Cornwall.

# COPYRIGHT

**interpreting the law
for libraries, archives and
information services**

# Contents

# Author's note

This book tries to set out the basics of UK copyright law, concentrating on those areas that may affect librarians and archivists in their daily work. There are many subjects that have not been dealt with at length, such as public performance, and aspects of broadcasting and publishing; and the whole area of design and patents is left to others far more competent than me to deal with them in those areas where they impinge on the work of libraries. Neither is it intended as a scholarly textbook but rather as a working tool for the practitioner who is faced with actual situations that need to be resolved in an informed and sensible way. References to case law or even specific clauses of the legislation are therefore not included. The book can be used as a desktop reference work for anyone planning library, archive and information services or kept at the enquiry desk to help decide what can, or cannot, be done for a reader. The author's hope is that it will be as helpful to junior counter staff as to senior managers. It is also aimed at all types of library, archive and information service, whether public, academic, government or private. Attention is given to the different legal situations in which various libraries function. As would be expected, the book focuses on UK law, which it aims to interpret, and the answers found here should never be assumed to apply in other countries. Nevertheless, many of the questions raised are equally valid in any part of the world and should help professionals in other countries to address the issues facing their own libraries.

As libraries, archives and information providers increasingly move towards exploiting their collections or providing new information resources, there is a need to look at what rights libraries and others enjoy when they create a work as well as when they wish to use something. Digitization programmes in particular raise many challenging questions and some of these will be dealt with in this book.

It is organized on a question-and-answer pattern to simplify searching for particular problems and their possible solutions. Because of this there is a small amount of repetition between sections. This is quite deliberate to avoid unnecessary 'see also' comments, which tend to confuse or bewilder the user. Obviously not every possible question can be answered but every effort has been made to anticipate those that arise most often. The feedback from many users of previous editions of this book has been most useful in expanding and amplifying some of the paragraphs in this new edition. The law is not there to deal in specific terms with any and every possible situation but to provide the framework within which decisions can be made in specific circumstances. There are always 'grey' areas of interpretation or circumstance when the law will be unclear. Where this is the case, the book tries to offer guidance rather than provide a definite answer as this is not always possible. Although some of the legislation is still very new, other elements have been in place long enough to make it possible to give some further guidance in areas that were 'fuzzy' when the first edition was prepared in 1989. It should be remembered that what the law does not allow can often be done with the copyright owner's consent through an appropriate licence. Therefore, where the book says that the law prevents something, librarians and archivists should first check to see what kind of licence, if any, their institution holds for copying beyond the stated limits. For this reason a chapter on licences has been included in the sure and certain knowledge that it will soon become out of date in such a fast-moving area. In a book of this kind it is not possible to say exactly what existing licences allow as they differ between different kinds of institution and will change with time but general indications have been given as guidance.

The author advised the British Library on copyright matters for 18 years and took part in many of the discussions that helped to shape the library profession's reaction to the new law and the many statutory instruments that have followed the main legislation. He was involved in many similar discussions in Brussels and Luxembourg when the EU introduced a series of directives that have profoundly changed some aspects of UK law. He has served on a number of groups and committees dealing with copyright matters and has lectured and run seminars on copyright law both in the UK and abroad. He was also involved in a number of initiatives designing and implementing Electronic Copyright Management Systems (ECMS), which are already playing a major role in the future development of information work worldwide. He now works as an independent advisor and trainer in all aspects of copyright under the label ©opyright Circle. The wealth of information and opinion gathered from these contacts has been used to compile this book but it must be remembered that it is written by a librarian trying to understand the law, not a lawyer trying to understand libraries!

Graham P. Cornish
©opyright Circle
Harrogate

## Disclaimer

While the advice and information contained in this book are believed to be true and accuarate at the date of going to press, neither the author nor CILIP can accept any legal responsibility or liability for any errors or omissions that may be made.

# Acknowledgements

Nobody knows everything about copyright. Consequently, anyone who writes a book on the subject must be indebted to others working in the field. This is certainly true of this author and I would like to thank particularly my friend and sparring partner Sandy Norman who was Copyright Adviser to The Library Association, later CILIP, and for some time fulfilled a similar role for IFLA; Tim Padfield of The National Archives for his wisdom on every aspect of archives; Charles Oppenheim of Loughborough University for his challenging alternative interpretations of the law; and, above all, the many people who have taken part in the numerous copyright workshops throughout the country at which I have taught and whose questions have so enriched this edition.

My special thanks go to Stella Pilling, who has proofread the whole text and made many corrections and useful suggestions for improving it.

# List of abbreviations

AACR2   Anglo-American Cataloguing Rules Second Edition
ALCS    Authors' Licensing and Collecting Society
BLDSC   British Library Document Supply Centre
BNB     British National Bibliography
BPI     British Phonographic Industry
BSI     British Standards Institution
CBI     Confederation of British Industry
CCC     Copyright Clearance Center
CLA     Copyright Licensing Agency
DACS    Design and Artists Copyright Society
EEA     European Economic Area
ERA     Educational Recording Agency
HEI     higher education institution
HMSO    Her Majesty's Stationery Office
ILL     interlibrary loan
ISP     internet service provider
MCPS    Mechanical Copyright Protection Society

| | |
|---|---|
| NHS | National Health Service |
| NLA | Newspaper Licensing Agency |
| OCLC | Online Computer Library Center |
| OCR | optical character recognition |
| OHP | overhead projector |
| OS | Ordnance Survey |
| OU | Open University |
| OUEE | Open University Educational Enterprises |
| PLR | Public Lending Right |
| PPL | Phonographic Performance Ltd |
| PRS | Performing Right Society |
| SI | statutory instrument |
| SWPA | Spoken Word Publishers Association |
| UCC | Universal Copyright Convention |
| USGPO | United States Government Printing Office |
| VAT | value added tax |
| VIP | visually impaired person |
| VLE | virtual learning environment |
| WIPO | World Intellectual Property Organization |

# Introduction

The 1988 Copyright Act ('the Act' or 'the 1988 Act'), and the many subsequent statutory instruments that interpret and modify it, differs substantially from the one of 1956. However, some aspects of the 1956 Act still apply to some materials so it should not be ignored completely. Many definitions have changed, new rights have been introduced, lending and rental now play a much more prominent role in the law as it relates to libraries than previously and the new right of communication to the public needs careful scrutiny. Licensing as a concept is now also a major feature of information delivery but it was in its infancy in 1988.

The introduction of new legislation often has the effect of heightening awareness of the subject, making people more keen to know their rights and privileges and generally creating an atmosphere of extreme caution in case anyone puts a foot wrong and ends up in court. Although this is a good thing, nobody should become too paranoid. There has been a recent tendency for copyright infringement cases to be heard in criminal courts, but this is usually where important commercial considerations apply such as republishing or reproduction in bulk for commercial purposes. Criminal proceedings may also be taken for circumventing or tampering with electronic rights management systems. Most infringements of copyright by individuals are dealt with through the civil courts so that the rights owner must take legal proceedings if it is thought an infringement has taken place. As there are no cases at present involving libraries it would be reasonable to assume that a similar route would be taken, given that libraries are not, or should not be, involved in mass reproduction for commercial gain!

The Act and its supplementary legislation also set the stage for a completely new approach to the use of copyright material. We all know what the law says (even if we do not always know what it means!) so there is now the necessity to develop services outside the exceptions that the Copyright Act makes by talking to the licensing agencies and other rights owners' organizations to negotiate use of material in return for royalties. Those working in the information industries should not lose sight of this as a real way forward when the law inhibits the introduction of new services without the owners' consent. Licences granted by copyright owners can also override the limitations set by the law.

This fourth edition of *Copyright* takes account of the very latest legislation aimed at implementing the EU Directive on Copyright in the Information Society. New topics covered include copying for commercial use, the meaning of broadcasting and its implications for websites, electronic rights management and changes to educational copyright. Implications of the latest case law are considered. There is an extensive index, a list of useful addresses and websites, and a further reading list. The latter needs to be approached with caution as many standard works have not yet appeared in new editions taking the major changes in the law into account.

# Definition and law

**1**    **What is copyright?**
The idea behind copyright is rooted in certain fundamental ideas
about creativity and possession. Basically, it springs from the
idea that anything we create is an extension of 'self' and should
be protected from general use by anyone else. Coupled with this
is the idea that the person creating something has exclusive
rights over the thing created, partly for economic reasons but
also because of this extension of 'self' idea. Copyright is therefore important to ensure the continued growth of writing, performing and creating. If there were no copyright protection there
would be little stimulus for people to create anything, as other
people would be able to take the work and use it in any way they
wanted. Copyright law aims to protect this growth but, at the
same time, tries to ensure that some access to copyright works is
allowed as well. Without this access creators would be starved of
ideas and information to create more copyright material.

**2   Why is copyright important for libraries and archives?**

Libraries are in a unique position as custodians of copyright material. They have the duty to care for, and allow access to, other people's copyright works. This places special responsibilities on all those working in libraries, archives and the information world generally. We practise our profession by using this property so we should take all possible steps to protect it, while at the same time ensuring that the rights and privileges of our users and our profession are also safeguarded. Because copyright is such an intangible thing, there is often a temptation to ignore it. Those who take this approach forget that they, too, own copyright in their own creations and would feel quite angry if this were abused by others. Some of the restrictions placed on use by the law may seem petty or trivial but they are designed to allow some use of copyright material without unduly harming the interests of the creator (author).

**3   Is copyright valuable in terms of money?**

In the UK copyright is primarily a property right intended to protect the rights of those who create works of various kinds. The protection is to prevent exploitation of their works by others. It follows that copyright cannot exist by itself but only within the work that has been created. For this reason we say that copyright 'subsists' rather than exists.

**4   So, copyright is just about cash?**

No, authors also need to protect their personal rights, regardless of money. These rights are outlined in Section 3.

**5   What is the latest legislation?**

There are two acts of Parliament that are crucial to copyright. These are the Copyright, Designs and Patents Act (CDPA) 1988, which came into force on 1 August 1989, and the Copyright (Visually Impaired Persons) Act 2002, which came into force on 31 October 2003. The CDPA has to be read in conjunction with a number of subsequent statutory instruments and the support-ing regulations. There are a number of these but the statutory instruments (SIs) that affect libraries and archives most are:

SI 89/816 Copyright, Designs and Patents Act 1988 (Com-mencement No.1) Order

SI 89/1012 Copyright (Recordings of Folksongs for Archives) (Designated Bodies) Order

SI 89/1067 Copyright (Application of Provisions relating to Educational Establishments to Teachers) (No.2) Order

SI 89/1068 Copyright (Educational Establishments) (No.2) Order

SI 89/1098 The Copyright (Material Open to Public Inspection) (International Organizations) Order

SI 89/1099 The Copyright (Material Open to Public Inspection) (Making of Copies of Maps) Order

SI 89/1212 Copyright (Librarians and Archivists) (Copying of Copyright Materials) Regulations

SI 90/2510 The Copyright (Recording for Archives of Designated Class of Broadcasts and Cable Programmes) (Designated Bodies) (No.2) Order

SI 92/3233 Copyright (Computer Programs) Regulations 1992

SI 95/3297 Copyright Rights in Performances: the Duration of Copyright and Rights in Performances Regulations 1995

SI 96/2967 Copyright and Related Rights Regulations 1996

SI 97/3032 Copyright and Rights in Databases Regulations 1997

SI 99/1751 The Copyright (Application to Other Countries) Order 1999 as amended by SI 2003/774

SI 2003/188 The Copyright (Certification of Licensing Scheme for Educational Recording of Broadcasts and Cable Pro-grammes) (Educational Recording Agency Limited) (Amend-ment) Order 2003

SI 2003/2498 Copyright and Related Rights Regulations 2003.

Note that the texts of all this legislation can be found on the HMSO website, so extracts are not reproduced in this book. Go to www.legislation.hmso.gov.uk/acts.htm for the text of acts of Parliament; go to www.legislation.hmso.gov.uk/stat.htm for statutory instruments. In both cases click on the year concerned and find acts by alphabetical title or SIs by number. It is important to note that a number of defective statutory instruments were drawn up and never implemented. Other SIs with the same title but different numbering were replaced by those listed and the earlier ones should be ignored. This also applies to some SIs that became out of date and were effectively updated with replacements. It should also be noted that a number of terms used in the legislation are not defined. Most of these will be dealt with in the following text but include: original, substantial (and substantially), reasonable (and reasonably), librarian, fair dealing and periodical.

**6     Does the law apply to the whole of the UK?**

Yes, but remember that the Isle of Man and the Channel Islands are not part of the UK. Most (but not quite all) of the 1988 Act does not apply to the Channel Islands, which are still subject to either the 1956 Act or even parts of the 1911 Act. The Isle of Man passed its own copyright legislation in 1991 so that the copyright part of this Act (Part 1) does not apply there. The Manx legislation is sufficiently similar to UK law not to cause major problems. Also the Isle of Man is now covered by the database legislation. In addition, some aspects of remedies for owners relating to infringement and some of the criminal aspects of copyright are handled differently in Scotland because of the different way that Scots law works in these areas. It is to be hoped users of this book never have to investigate these!

**7     If I have all this legislation in front of me, can I work out what the law means?**

No! In addition to the many statutory instruments, you need to bear in mind that the language in the Act is full of undefined terms and that case law frequently changes the way we understand the meaning of the Act.

**8      Which terms are undefined?**
The following words and phrases crop up frequently but are never defined: commercial research, fair dealing, librarian, original, periodical, reasonable (and reasonably), substantial (and substantially).

**9      Any other catches?**
Yes, some phrases and words mean different things in different parts of the law. For example 'making available to the public' has several different meanings, as does 'publish'.

# 2

# What is covered by copyright?

**10  What things are covered by copyright?**

Virtually anything that is written, recorded in any form, or anything that can be made by a human being, but not usually things made by a mechanical process. The law divides these items into various classes and all aspects of them are dealt with separately in the following pages.

**11  Does absolutely anything in these groups qualify for copyright?**

No. There are three tests to qualify for copyright and any work must pass all three. They are that the work must be original, recorded and created by a qualifying person.

**12  What does 'original' mean?**

The law does not say, but the idea is that, to be protected, the author must have contributed quite a lot of their own ideas or skills to the making of the work.

*Example*: If you write your own poem about Jack and Jill, it is protected. If you simply reproduce the well-known nursery rhyme with one or two minor changes, that is not original and not protected (but the typographical arrangement may be (see paragraph 133 onwards). Works that are merely trivial will not qualify as they are not original.

**13    When does a work become original?**
When sufficient time, effort, technical skills and knowledge have been used to make it reasonably clear that the work is a new one and not merely a slavish copy.

**14    What about digitization and the images that produces?**
This is an area where the law is unclear. Generally speaking, it is held that if the work is digitized using a scanner and there is no human intervention (like a photocopy), then there is unlikely to be any new copyright work created. So a mere scanned copy may not be protected by copyright, but an image that has had a lot of work done on it to enhance its appearance, correct the text or change the colouring probably will be protected.

**15    So, if the library digitizes some old parts of its collection, can it benefit at all from copyright?**
If the images are enhanced, probably. But even if they are not, the actual collection of images may qualify for database right (see Section 9) if they are organized in a systematic and methodical way.

**16    What constitutes trivial?**
This is not defined but a primitive doodle or a simple 'x' would not qualify although what is 'simple' and what is not is open to debate!

**17    What does 'recorded' mean?**
Fixed in some way such as writing on paper, stored in a com-

puter system, recorded on a disc (vinyl, CD, CD-ROM) or on a film. A live performance, which is not recorded or videoed, for example, would not attract copyright.

**18    Can copyright subsist even if the original work has disappeared or been destroyed?**

Yes. If, for example, a painting was photographed and then destroyed, there would still be copyright in the original painting, even though it did not exist, through the existence of the photograph.

**19    Which authors qualify for copyright protection?**

The person claiming to be the author must be a UK citizen or a citizen of a country where UK works are protected in the same way as in Britain (see paragraph 708 and following). A complete list of these countries is given in the statutory instruments listed in Section 1. Also anyone carrying out work for the Crown, Parliament, the United Nations or the Organization of American States has that work protected as if it were published in the UK, even if the author is a national of a country not otherwise covered by these arrangements. See also paragraph 45.

**20    Is the title of a book or journal article protected by copyright?**

Rarely. Such titles are statements of fact – they tell you what the book or article is called – and cannot therefore be protected unless they are so complex that they become a literary work in their own right or are registered as a trademark. In this case the problem would arise only if the 'make-up' of the new work looked so like the first work that one could be mistaken for the other. How many journals called *Impact* or *Update* do you know?

**21    Is there copyright in facts?**

No. A fact is a fact and cannot be protected as such. However, the way in which information about facts is presented is protected.

*Example*: Times of trains are facts and nobody can prevent you from publishing information that trains leave at certain times for particular places. What is protected is the layout of the timetable and the actual typography. So you might make this information available by including it in a brochure about a tourist attraction but it would be an infringement to photocopy the timetable and reprint this in the brochure.

## 22 What about works which are illegal, such as pornography?

Just because a work is pornographic, libelous or irreligious this does not mean it is not protected by copyright. On the other hand, courts have sometimes refused to uphold copyright in such works where a claim for infringement has occurred. The problem is, as always in such matters, what is pornographic today may be entirely acceptable tomorrow. Thus there will be copyright in such works but it may be difficult to enforce.

## 23 Are things like trademarks and logos protected by copyright?

Yes. A logo is an artistic work and a trademark may well be an artistic work and/or a literary work as well. It is quite possible for a trademark to go out of copyright but still be a trademark as trademarks can last indefinitely. Therefore it could be allowed to copy an old trademark provided it was not used in such a way that it was not also used as a trademark. For example, it might be possible to illustrate a book on advertising with pictures of out-of-copyright trademarks provided they are just pictures and not used to market a product.

## 24 Are any works excepted from the usual copyright protection?

Yes. The Bible, the Book of Common Prayer (BCP) of the Church of England and Sir James Barrie's *Peter Pan* all enjoy special protection outside normal copyright limitations. The

Authorized Version of the Bible and the BCP are printed under patents issued by the Crown and are therefore in perpetual copyright. This does not extend to modern versions, which must be treated as published works that are anonymous, whatever one's personal theological view! The Authorized Version of the Bible and BCP cannot be copied as they are outside copyright law. Permission is usually given for small quotations in published versions and photocopying of various portions for research or private study or for reading in church or chapel is usually allowed. In the case of *Peter Pan*, the Copyright Act brought in perpetual copyright in this play for the benefit of the Hospital for Sick Children, Great Ormond Street, London, provided it remains a hospital. The Hospital owned the copyright, which expired on 31 December 1987 and obtained a considerable revenue from it. Parliament decided to continue this privilege and any commercial publication or performance of the work attracts a royalty for the Hospital. This is a form of compulsory licensing for a work now out of copyright. As the Act did not come into force until 1 August 1989 any act of copying, commercial publication or performance done between 31 December 1987 and 31 July 1989 was not an infringement. The play cannot be publicly performed without royalty payment to the Hospital for Sick Children. However, as these arrangements are very similar to those for revived copyright (see paragraph 44), it is unclear which regulations will take precedence, should they differ, during the period of revived copyright, which will last until 2007. In addition, some items, such as patents, qualify technically for copyright, but an international agreement between patent offices has waived all protection of patents for non-commercial copying.

# Rights and limitations

Authors and owners may or may not be the same person. They enjoy different rights so this distinction is important. As authors are defined differently for different types of work, they will be dealt with separately under each heading. However, despite some variations, their moral rights are similar in all circumstances so they will be covered in this section, which sets out who the owner is and what the owner is entitled to do exclusively in law. However, all rights also have limitations in order to exercise them, so the law limits these exclusive rights in a number of ways and this section should be interpreted in the light of what is said later about other people being allowed to do certain acts as well. It is these exceptions that form the bulk of this book.

## Moral rights

### 25  What are moral rights?

Moral rights are designed to protect the idea that anything created contains an element of 'self' in it. Therefore the author ought to be able to protect certain aspects of a work. The law is complex in this area and most library services will not have major concerns with moral rights so no attempt is made to give an exhaustive description of them.

**26    What are these rights?**
Essentially they give the author of a work the right not to have the work subjected to derogatory treatment.

**27    What constitutes derogatory treatment?**
Basically, authors have the right to prevent their work being distorted by additions, deletions or changes to its meaning. They also have the right not to have works they did not create attributed to them.

**28    What about making sure their name is included in a work?**
This is not, surprisingly, an automatic right of the author. It applies in certain contexts only and will be dealt with under each type of copyright material in the following sections.

**29    Do moral rights last for the same length of time?**
Yes, but with one important exception. The right not to have works falsely attributed to oneself lasts for only 20 years from the end of the year in which the person dies.

## Ownership of copyright

**30    What is ownership of copyright?**
Ownership of copyright is complex. Copyright is a property and can be disposed of in the same way as other property, so ownership is not always easy to identify. The author may have assigned the copyright to someone else. It may have been sold to a publisher, given to someone else, left to someone in a will or automatically transferred to an employer, the Crown or Parliament.

In 1996 the law changed, extending copyright protection in many cases from 50 to 70 years after death. This gave rise to 'extended' copyright (where 20 years have been added on to existing copyright) and 'revived' copyright (where a work was out of copyright because the author had been dead for more than 50 years but, because he or she had been dead for fewer than 70 years, copyright came back into force).

**31   Is the copyright in a work one single piece of property or can it be broken up?**

Copyright is a complicated bundle of rights (see paragraph 48) and these can be assigned or licensed to different people. They can also be licensed for a limited period so that one person may have one bundle of rights for ten years, then acquire a licence for them for a further 30 years and so on. This is particularly important for works made into films or plays, musicals, operas and ballets.

**32   Are there any rules for transferring copyright?**

Yes, an assignment of copyright (by which the owner passes over their rights for ever) must be in writing; an agreement to allow someone else to use the work for, say, ten years is a licence and need not be in writing.

**33   Someone must start the ownership process. Who owns copyright first?**

Copyright is usually owned first of all by the author.

**34   Why usually?**

Because there are different rules depending on employment or commissioning.

**35   How does employment come into ownership?**

If authors create a work as part of their job, then their employer is usually the owner. However, there can be a contract between employer and employee, which can state the opposite (that the copyright remains with the employee). See the notes on commissioned works in the following paragraphs. There are special arrangements for Crown and Parliamentary copyright (see paragraph 45 and following). Also the author is differently defined for different classes of works such as films and sound recordings. Most of the legislation is actually about the rights enjoyed by the owner of copyright rather than the author. For this reason most authors' economic rights are referred to as 'owner's rights'.

## 36 Supposing the work was commissioned?

If the work was commissioned after 1 August 1989 the copyright is owned by the author. Before that date, copyright in commissioned paintings, engravings and photographs is usually the property of the person who paid for the commission. Copyright in other types of commissioned works remains with the person creating the work.

## 37 Does 'commissioned' mean the author had to be paid?

Yes, but this is important now only for artistic works mentioned in paragraph 391, commissioned before 1 August 1989.

## 38 Supposing a library owns an original work such as a manuscript. Does the library own the copyright?

No. It is important to distinguish between the object and the copyright, which subsists in it. The library may own the manuscript but the copyright is still owned by the author or the person to whom it has been assigned, so the library has no right to reproduce the manuscript, except as allowed by the exceptions in the Copyright Act. However, the library may enjoy other rights over the manuscript under publication right (see paragraphs 135 to 141). When a library or archive has material bequeathed to it through the will of the original author it is assumed that the copyright also becomes the property of the library or archive unless the owner stipulated otherwise.

**39   Who owns the copyright in a letter?**

The author, that is, the person who wrote the letter.

**40   Why does the person who received the letter not own it?**

Because copyright belongs to the person who creates the work. The letter itself does belong to the person who received it. They were given it by the writer. But the copyright still belongs to the writer, not the recipient of the letter.

**41   What about a letter sent to the editor of a newspaper or journal?**

Technically the copyright still belongs to the writer of the letter although, by sending the letter to the editor in the first place, there is an assumption that the writer wished it to be published and therefore the editor has an implied licence to publish. This does not give the editor or the publisher any other rights over the use of the letter.

**42   Who owns the copyright in a periodical issue?**

Each author of an article in a periodical issue owns the copyright in that article but the publisher owns the copyright in the issue as a whole, including the typographical arrangement (see paragraph 134).

*Example*: Someone writes an article for a periodical. Unless they sign an agreement to the contrary, they retain the copyright in the article and have the right to have it published elsewhere. But they do not have the right simply to photocopy the article as first published and have it republished in that form. This would infringe the typographical copyright of the publisher. Nor do they have the right to make copies of the whole periodical issue. For the same reason, the author cannot simply make multiple photocopies of the article for friends and colleagues.

**43   Who owns 'extended copyright'?**

Essentially the person who owned the copyright immediately

before the extended copyright came into force (see paragraph 30).

## 44   Who owns 'revived' copyright?

The person who owned the copyright immediately before it expired. If that person is dead, or the body owning the copyright has ceased to exist, then the copyright is owned by the personal representatives of the author (see paragraph 30).

## 45   Who owns Crown Copyright?

Technically, the Crown. However, Crown Copyright is administered by HMSO, which, although now privatized, still has a residual responsibility to administer copyright owned by the Crown.

## 46   Who owns the copyright in a Parliamentary bill or act of Parliament?

The copyright in a bill belongs to whichever House introduced the bill first. When the bill becomes an act it becomes Crown Copyright.

## 47   Supposing a work is out of print. Does the publisher still own the copyright?

This will depend on the contract between the author and the publisher but, generally speaking, copyright in a work reverts to the author if the work goes out of print and the publisher has no plans to reprint or republish the work. However, the publisher will retain the copyright in the typography of the work (see paragraph 133 and following).

## 48   What rights does the law give the copyright owner?

Copyright law gives the owner exclusive rights to do certain things to or with the copyright material. Nobody else is entitled to do these things. There are seven basic rights:

• to copy the work
• to issue copies to the public

- to perform, show or play the work
- to adapt or translate the work
- to rent or lend the work
- to communicate the work to the public by electronic means
- to make the work available.

Each of these rights will be examined under the appropriate type of work. Those who own rights in databases or performances have quite different rights.

**49    Are these absolute rights or do other people have some rights to use the material as well?**
They are not absolute because they are limited by quantity, time, purpose and certain exemptions given to user groups. Each of these limitations will be examined under the appropriate type of work. But it is important to note that the limitations set for use of copyright material are exceptions to the rights of owners and not rights enjoyed by users.

## Quantity

**50    Is the whole and every little bit of a work protected?**
No. Copyright is limited by excluding from protection less than a substantial part of a work. So if less than a substantial part is used or copied there is no infringement except in certain areas.

**51    What constitutes a substantial part?**
Substantial is one of those undefined words. What is clear is that it is not just a question of quantity but of quality as well.
*Example*: Someone copies a page from a 250-page novel, it could be argued that this one page is not a substantial part of the whole work because it does not contain any important information about the story line or its setting. But, if it were the last page of a whodunit, which gave away the whole plot, then it would certainly be substantial. Someone else copies the recom-

mendations and conclusions (three paragraphs) from a 70-page technical report. This is almost certainly a substantial part. Similarly four bars of a symphony could constitute a substantial part because they encapsulate the theme music of the whole work.

**52   So are there any guidelines?**
Not really. Each case must be a matter of professional judgement.

## Time and purpose

**53   Does copyright last for ever?**
No, but the rules relating to how long it does last are very complex. They will be dealt with for each type of copyright material in the following sections.

**54   For what purposes can copyright material be used without asking permission?**
The law gives several main reasons:

- fair dealing
- public administration
- temporary copies.

These will be covered as each type of copyright material is discussed in the following sections.

## User groups

**55   Are any exceptions made for particular user groups or needs?**
The law gives special exceptions and privileges to three user groups:

- those working in or undertaking education
- libraries and their users
- visually impaired people.

These will also be discussed with each type of copyright material in the following sections.

# Literary, dramatic and musical works

These three classes are dealt with together because they are all treated in a similar way under the Copyright Act, although there are some differences for some specific areas. In addition, a printed text also has a copyright in the typographical arrangement of the work concerned, regardless of the copyright status of the content. Any literary work, which will also qualify as a database, is subject to special rules. See Section 9 for details.

## Definitions

### Literary works

**56    What is a literary work?**

The term 'literary work' includes anything that is printed or written such as books, journals, technical reports and manuscripts, and also covers any works that are spoken or sung. It also includes compilations (although how these differ from databases is a matter of debate) as well as computer programs and text stored electronically. For example, the words of a popular song are protected as a literary work; the music is treated separately (see paragraphs 63 to 65). The handwritten notes of an author are protected just as much as the final printed book.

**57 Does 'literary' mean it has to be good quality literature?**
No. Copyright law says almost nothing about the quality or content of the work although case law shows that trivial works are not eligible for protection. Literary means anything that is written, spoken or sung which has been recorded, whether in writing or some other way.

**58 What about databases? Are these covered by copyright?**
They may occasionally be covered by copyright but they are definitely covered by database right as a separate type of work. See Section 9 for details.

**59 Are bibliographic records covered by copyright?**
This is a difficult question and has never been clarified in law. The question is: Is a bibliographic record 'original'? Originality requires some intellectual input from the author. Most bibliographic records consist of a series of facts presented in a predetermined order according to AACR2 or another cataloguing code of practice. In theory, everyone using these codes should produce exactly the same record. It has been held that merely to follow exact instructions does not give the person actually doing the work any copyright in the work they create. For example, an architectural draughtsman following exact design instructions is not considered to have made a new copyright work. The fact that they do not is more to do with human fallibility than the rules themselves! But it could be argued that human intellect had been used to implement the rules. Therefore it would be difficult to decide whether a catalogue record has any copyright as such, although the typography in a published catalogue would be protected (see paragraph 134 and following).

**60   So are bibliographies not protected by copyright?**

Almost any bibliography will now qualify as a database rather than a literary work and must be treated accordingly. The one exception is the scholarly bibliography, which may be annotated and is prepared by one identifiable person. See Section 9 for detailed information.

**61   Is a library catalogue protected?**

A library catalogue is almost certainly a database and will be protected as such under copyright law. See Section 9.

## Dramatic works

**62   What is the difference between a literary and a dramatic work?**

A dramatic work is the non-spoken part of a presentation and includes dance and mime. The words of a dramatic work are protected as a literary work. For example, a show like West Side Story will have separate copyrights in the words (literary work), the choreography and directions (dramatic work) and the music (musical work).

## Musical works

**63   Does musical work mean anything with music included?**

No. Musical work means only the music and excludes the words (which are a literary work) and any actions, which go with the music because they are dramatic works.

*Example*: West Side Story (as mentioned above in 'dramatic works') will have three separate copyrights: in the words, in the actions and movements of the singers, and in the musical notes. Although this may sound complicated it is important because the people who composed the three elements will each own a separate copyright, which may expire at different times. So the music might go out of copyright but not the words, or vice versa.

**64   Does musical work include a recording of the music?**

No. That is separately covered as a sound recording (see Section 6).

**65   What about a play performed and recorded on video?**

The play is protected as a literary work and the video made of the performance is protected as a film, quite separately. The performers will also have separate rights in their performances.

**66   Definition of author**

It is important to define who the author of a work is as this will usually determine how long copyright lasts. Copyright is most often linked to the death of the author. It is also important to note that the author is defined differently for different types of material, but for literary, dramatic, musical and artistic works the definitions are more or less the same.

**67   What is the definition of the author?**

This varies according to the type of work being considered, but for literary, dramatic and musical works it is the person who created the work.

**68   Supposing there are two or more authors?**

They all count as the authors of the copyright.

**69   Supposing it is not possible to find out who the author is?**

A work is considered anonymous if the identity of the author cannot be traced by making reasonable enquiries.

**70   What does 'reasonable enquiry' mean?**

This is not defined but it would presumably require checking in major catalogues and relevant literary dictionaries, and so on.

**71   Supposing the author's identity is established later on?**

Once the author's identity is established, then the work is no longer anonymous and the usual procedures apply.

**72    Supposing the author has used a pseudonym?**

Unless you can find out whose pseudonym it is, then the work is counted as anonymous. Like anonymous works, this would require reasonable enquiry – checking of literary reference works and major library catalogues.

**73    What happens if a work definitely has more than one author, but not all their names are known?**

Once the name of even one author is known, the work is no longer anonymous.

*Example*: Title page of a book states: 'Love Poems by the author of "Love Songs" et al.' Once the authorship of 'Love Songs' has been established, the work is not anonymous, even though the identity of 'et al.' may never be known.

**74    Supposing the author is given as an organization?**

If no person is named as the author, the work is treated as anonymous.

**75    If a work was generated by a computer, who counts as the author then?**

The person who made the necessary arrangements for creating the work (but see Section 9).

**76    What about compilations such as directories, timetables, bibliographies and encyclopedias?**

If the work has a personal author then that is the author, so a bibliography compiled by someone is protected just as if it were a book. However, something like the *British National Bibliography* has no personal author so is protected only as a database. Most works like this will qualify as databases (see Section 9) for which separate rules apply.

**77   What about works that have lots of articles by different people, such as an encyclopedia?**
Then each article is protected as a separate work, and it may also be a database.

**78   Supposing some articles are signed and some not?**
They are all treated separately as individual works, so copyright in some will be treated as the work of an author and some will be anonymous.

## Authors' rights

**79   Do authors of literary, dramatic and musical works all enjoy moral rights?**
It depends on the type of material. Authors of monographs and directors of films have the author's name included when the work is published. This right has to be asserted in writing. Authors of other works in this group do not have this right. However, authors of works in this group do have the right to prevent derogatory treatment of their work (see paragraph 25 and following in Section 3).

## Owners' rights in literary, dramatic, and musical works

Essentially copyright is a monopoly against which certain exceptions are set to make a balance between owner and user. This section begins by looking at the rights that owners of copyright enjoy and then examining how they are limited by exceptions.

## Copying

**80   Does the owner alone have the right to make copies?**
Yes, subject to the limitations mentioned later on.

**81   Does copying just mean photocopying?**

Certainly not. It means copying in any material form. This includes any method of copying including, of course, resetting the type to make a new edition for publication, copying by hand or taking a photograph. Photocopying is clearly copying something and there are special provisions to allow some types of copying for some purposes. It also includes electronic copying and this includes storing a work in any form and copying the text onto a computer disc, converting it to electronically readable text using scanning equipment of various kinds, storing it on CD-ROM or transmitting it by fax. This also includes making copies of computer programs for any purpose.

**82   But using a computer, especially the internet, also involves copying. Is this not allowed either?**

The law gives the owner the exclusive right to control the making of copies that are transient or incidental to some other use of the work. This would mean that using the internet without permission would be an infringement!! However, the new legislation in 2003 takes away the right of the owner to prevent you making these temporary copies. See Section 11 for more details.

**83   Fax involves copying. Is the use of fax really an infringement?**

Given that the new law allows the making of temporary copies, which have no independent significance, it would seem likely that merely sending a fax which produced nothing more than a paper copy at the end would not be an infringement. However, if the process resulted in a stored electronic copy being generated and available for subsequent use, then this would probably be an infringement.

**84   Documents received by fax sometimes fade and disappear. Can the document be further copied as soon as it is received to make a durable copy?**

Not legally. Unlike the temporary copy made by a fax transmission, this is a permanent copy so further copies should not be made. An exception might be a copy faxed for interlibrary loan (ILL) purposes so that the faxed copy might be further copied for preservation purposes.

**85    What about microforms?**
Making a microform is copying and is not permitted without the owner's consent.

**86    Could catalogue records be photocopied and put into a library catalogue?**
No. Although each entry might well not attract copyright, there will certainly be copyright in the typography and by cutting up the photocopy and using the entries as catalogue cards this will infringe the typographical arrangement, as the use would not be for fair dealing. (The term 'fair dealing' is crucial to understanding much of this book – see paragraph 174 and following for more detailed information.)

**87    Can copies be made for committee meetings?**
No. Copying for committees is multiple copying and is not permitted unless the amount copied is less than substantial. However, in many organizations committee copying would be covered by an appropriate licence.

**88    Can a slide or overhead projector (OHP) be made of a page of a book for teaching in a class or giving a lecture?**
Not under the law. The British Copyright Council has said that copying for a 'one-off' lecture to, say, a local history group or for general classroom use, would not be regarded by them as an infringement. Alternatively, if less than a substantial part were copied then it would be in order to make a slide of that part.

**89    Some books and journals carry a warning that no part of the work can be reproduced, stored, etc. Does this take away the allowances given under the Copyright Act?**

This statement has never been tested in law. It is generally thought unlikely that it would stand up in court as it tries to prohibit what the law allows. There is an argument that it constitutes a contract between the publisher and the user about which the user knew perfectly well before buying the book but general opinion is that it is there to frighten rather than be enforced! Actual enforcement of it would be a very difficult thing to do and costly in legal fees to establish as binding. Of course, if it were binding, libraries could refuse to buy the books, which would make a considerable difference to publishers' sales. More recent books by properly informed publishers preface this prohibitive statement with the phrase 'Except as permitted by the 1988 Copyright, Designs and Patents Act . . .'.

## Issuing copies to the public

**90    Is issuing copies to the public the same as publishing?**

No, issuing copies to the public is much wider in scope. As well as publishing it includes rental and lending.

**91    If issuing copies to the public is an infringement, how can libraries offer a lending service?**

The law makes it clear that the right to issue copies to the public only applies to works not previously put into circulation in the European Economic Area (EEA). There are specific provisions for the lending and rental of copyright material (see 'lending and rental' under each type of material).

**92    Does this idea of issuing copies to the public have any bearing on acquisition of materials?**

Essentially, no. Any responsibility for infringing importation would rest with the bookseller involved, not the library. Libraries occasionally import single copies but these are not for commercial purposes so infringement is unlikely.

## Performing a work

**93 Who has the right to decide whether a work can be performed in public?**
Every author has the right to decide whether a work shall be performed in public, whether it is a recitation of a poem, extracts from a book, or delivery of a speech. The author also has the right to decide whether the performance can be recorded.

**94 Libraries and archives are not often involved in public performances. Is this really important for them?**
Libraries are increasingly involved in cultural activities and some have library theatres so it is important to be aware of the owner's rights, especially when library materials may be used to put on performances. This includes plays, concerts and arts festivals generally.

**95 Can only the copyright owner authorize performance?**
Yes, although it may be done through a licensing agency (see Section 10).

**96 Does performance mean just plays or presentations?**
No. Performance includes delivery of speeches, lectures or sermons and also includes presentation by visual or audible means.
*Example*: If the library possesses some poems by a local author, they may not be copied. But it is also an infringement to recite them in public or make a video of someone reciting them in public. Family videos of weddings, for example, may infringe the copyright in the vicar's sermon if reading from a prepared text. However, if the vicar is speaking extempore, there is no copyright in the sermon until it has been recorded (on the video).

The vicar then owns the copyright in the sermon and the person who shot the video owns the copyright in the video as such!

**97   Does this mean that poems cannot be used for public recitation?**

Not quite. One person may read a reasonable extract from a copyright work in public provided that the reading is accompanied by sufficient acknowledgement.

**98   What do the terms 'reasonable extract' and 'sufficient acknowledgement' mean?**

They are not defined. Reasonable extract is a matter of judgement. Sufficient acknowledgement would certainly mean saying who wrote the work, when and where it was published, if published at all.

**99   What about story-telling for children in libraries?**

Technically this is an infringement by performance (see Section 10).

**100   Sometimes teachers want to perform plays or hold concerts using copyright library materials. Is this allowed?**

Yes, provided that only pupils, teachers and other persons directly connected with the educational establishment are present. This does not include mums and dads!

## Communicating the work by electronic means

**101   What exactly does this mean in practical terms?**

This right is a new one and is defined as 'Communication to the public by electronic transmission', which includes:

* broadcasting the work
* making the work available by electronic transmission so that

members of the public may access it from a place and at a time individually chosen by them.

This clearly includes putting material on a website and therefore compensates for the earlier definition of a broadcast, which specifically excluded websites and internet transmission. See Section 8 for broadcasts.

However, if the work is also transmitted via the internet at the same time it is broadcast or if the transmission is by internet only but at a time chosen solely by the person making the transmission (in other words using the internet as a broadcasting medium) then this is regarded as broadcasting and not communicating the work to the public by electronic means. In a nutshell, broadcasting takes precedence over internet transmission when determining the status of a transmitted work.

## 102  Does this have any implications for libraries and archives?

As far as literary, dramatic or musical works go, the main fact to bear in mind is that broadcasting a work is an infringement of the owner's rights. So if a local radio station wished to use some of the library's holdings for broadcasting purposes, such as poems, musical compositions or extracts from local history material, this would not be allowed without permission. This would not apply if the use were solely for news reporting.

## 103  Does this have any effect on the use of websites?

Yes. The definition of this right makes it clear that putting anything on a website without the copyright owner's permission is an infringement.

## Adaptation and translation

## 104  Does adaptation apply just to plays, novels or similar materials?

No. It includes translation, adaptation, conversion of dramatic works to non-dramatic works and turning a story into a cartoon or similar work. Translating a work is considered an adaptation and translations should not be made without due consideration for the purpose for which they are made and the use to which they will be put.

**105 What can be done for a researcher in a laboratory who needs a technical article translated?**

As the use would be for a commercial purpose, the translation can be made only with the consent of the copyright owner.

**106 What about a student who wants to translate a play in a foreign language?**

If the student makes their own translation there is unlikely to be a problem as copying by non-mechanical means in the course of instruction is permitted (see paragraph 208 and following). It would be interesting to test the exception if an automatic translating program were used!

## Dramatic and non-dramatic works

**107 It is an infringement to re-write a non-dramatic work as a dramatic one and vice-versa. Is it also an infringement to reproduce a story in another form such as pictures?**

*Example*: Someone decides to re-work Alan Ayckbourn's *The Norman Conquests* as a novel. This is an infringement. Equally it would be an infringement to produce a dramatic version of one of Catherine Cookson's novels.

**108 Does this restriction include turning a story into pictures, for example for a children's library?**

Yes. The law specifies that it is not allowed to turn the story into a version wholly or mainly told in the form of pictures suitable for reproduction in a book, newspaper or magazine. Although this is obviously aimed at the cartoon market, it has implications for children's libraries and school libraries as well.

**109 How does this affect arrangements of musical works?**
Any arrangement or transcription of a musical work counts as an adaptation.

**110 Does 'translation' extend to computer languages?**
Yes. The law specifically states that changing a program from one computer language to another is an infringement unless this is done incidentally during the running of the program. But see Section 9.

**111 Supposing an adaptation or translation has been made quite legally. Does that also attract copyright?**
Yes, and the person who made the adaptation has rights in the adaptation just as the author has in the original work.

## Lending and rental

**112 What about lending and rental?**
Under the 1988 Act lending and rental of certain materials became an exclusive right of the copyright owner. In 1996 this right was extended to all materials. However, the rules are complicated and libraries enjoy certain specific privileges as listed below.

**113 What is actually meant by 'lending'?**
The meaning of 'lending' is defined in the new legislation as follows:

• that a work is made available for use on the presumption that it will, or may be, returned
• the lending does not lead to any economic or commercial advantage to the lender

- the lending is done by an establishment that is accessible to the public OR by a prescribed library (see paragraph 302 and following) that is not conducted for profit BUT by a public library only if the work is covered by the Public Lending Right Act or was acquired before 1 December 1996.

Lending does not include:

- making available for public performance
- performing in public
- broadcasting
- making available for exhibition purposes
- on-the-spot reference use
- making available between establishments accessible to the public.

**114   Does this mean that a library that lends material cannot charge?**
No. The necessary operating costs of the lending establishment may be recovered. Where lending takes place in these conditions it is not defined as 'lending'!

**115   What does 'on-the-spot' mean?**
This is not defined but it would seem clear that use of a work within a library or similar collection where the work is not taken out of the room would clearly be on-the-spot. Whether taking a work from one room in a building to another or from one building to another within a single site still constitutes on-the-spot is not clear. It seems unlikely that 'the spot' would be stretched to use on a different site.

**116   Which libraries can lend material?**
As educational establishments can lend any material it would seem likely that the library of any such establishment could lend material to another library.

**117  What about other libraries?**
Any library that is a prescribed library (see paragraph 302 and following) and which is not conducted for profit can lend material, so presumably it can be lent to other libraries.

**118  What about public libraries?**
As public libraries can lend only books within the Public Lending Right (PLR) scheme they can lend only these items to other libraries.

**119  What can public libraries lend?**
After 1 December 1996 public libraries can lend:

- any printed materials obtained before 1 December 1996
- only materials acquired after 1 December 1996 that are covered by the Public Lending Right scheme or which would have been eligible for coverage by the scheme because of their form, but are precluded because of country of origin, date of the author's death, or other similar reasons.

To try to clarify this, a new edition of a book by an author who died over 70 years ago is not eligible for PLR but would have been if the author had died recently. To avoid the situation where the public library could not lend this book because it is outside the PLR scope, it can be treated for lending as if it is eligible even though it is not!

**120  What about books without authors such as directories or bibliographies?**
These can be for reference only, if acquired after 1 December 1996.

**121  What about periodicals, maps, or photographs?**
If acquired after 1 December 1996 they must be for reference only.

**122  What about lending works through interlibrary loan?**
Care may be needed here. Lending between establishments that
are accessible to the public is not counted as lending. But there
are special clauses dealing with libraries that will probably override this general exception, since normal practice is that where
specific regulations exist they take precedence over general rules.

**123  Can any library take part in these arrangements?**
It depends whether the library is being asked for copies or is asking for copies and whether the library wishes to lend or borrow.

**124  Which libraries can lend to other libraries?**
There is no legislation that deals directly with lending between
libraries. 'Lending' is defined as not including 'making available
between establishments which are accessible to the public' but:

• the term 'accessible to the public' is not defined
• there are separate clauses for lending from libraries which are
  not just establishments accessible to the public.

However, some possible situations in which interlibrary loan can
take place can be deduced.

**125  What do these special arrangements permit?**
These allow any prescribed library (see paragraph 302 for a definition of this term) that is not conducted for profit to lend copyright works. As lending is defined as not being for economic or
commercial gain, the charging for this interlending should not
cost more than the operating costs to carry out the lending. So a
commercial or industrial library cannot lend but they can borrow such items from other non-profit prescribed libraries.

**126  If a work has been borrowed by a library can it then be
lent to the end-user?**
It would seem that this will depend on whether that library can

lend this type of material to end-users from its own collection. If lending from its own collection would not be allowed, it is unlikely that a library could lend material from another collection of the sort that it could not lend from its own collection. For example, public libraries cannot lend issues of periodicals so it would seem unlikely that a public library could borrow a back issue from another library (say an educational library) and lend that to the end-user when it cannot lend the same type of material from its own collection.

**127    What about libraries in commerce and industry?**
As the law stands a library in this category cannot lend any material but it might be able to borrow from other libraries. However, it would not be able to lend the material borrowed as such libraries are not allowed to lend.

**128    What constitutes rental?**
Rental is making something available for a limited time on the expectation that it will be returned and for which a charge above the necessary operating costs is recovered.

**129    Can libraries have rental schemes?**
Only with the agreement of the copyright owner.

## Crown and Parliamentary copyright

**130    What is Crown Copyright?**
When a work is created by an employee of the Crown it becomes subject to Crown Copyright, which is technically owned by the Crown (Her Majesty), and different rules apply to this type of material.

**131    Who counts as a Crown employee?**
Since the distancing of much civil service work from central government and recent moves to devolution this is no longer clear.

Staff at major government departments and ministries are Crown employees but the status of many bodies (for example the British Library) is unclear.

### 132   What is Parliamentary copyright?
Parliamentary copyright exists in any work commissioned by either or both Houses of Parliament.

## Typographical arrangements of published editions

### 133   What is typographical copyright?
Every published work has two copyrights: one in the actual content of the text and the other in the printed layout of the page.

### 134   Who counts as the author of the typographical arrangement of a work?
The publisher.

## Publication right

### 135   What is publication right?
Publication right is a new right introduced on 1 December 1996. It is similar to, but distinct from, copyright as such.

### 136   Does publication right exist in all works?
No, but it can exist in any library, dramatic, musical or artistic work, or a film.

### 137   So when does it exist?
Publication right exists when anyone in the European Economic Area (EEA) first publishes a work that is:

* out of copyright
* published by someone who is an EEA citizen
* has not been published in the UK or any EEA state.

**138 Does 'published' mean published commercially?**

No. In the context of publication right (and the definition is different in different contexts) it means communication to the public (an undefined term) and in particular:

- issue of copies to the public
- making the work available by means of an electronic retrieval system
- rental or lending of copies to the public
- performance, showing or exhibiting in public
- broadcasting including cable.

**139 When does an unpublished work go out of copyright?**

See paragraph 154 and following for details. Note that unpublished literary, dramatic and musical works of which the author had died before 1 January 1969 are protected for 50 years from that the date when the new law came into force (i.e. 1989) and therefore do not come out of copyright until 2039, the first date on which publication right for these classes of works can come into force. Unpublished works of an author who died after 31 December 1968 enjoy the usual 70 years protection unless the author is a national of a non-EEA country, in which case copyright lasts for as long as that country provides protection.

**140 Does this mean that, where publication right comes into force, libraries and archives lose control of unpublished material in their collections?**

Fortunately, no. The publication can take place only with the consent of the owner of the physical material in which the work is recorded. So a library or archive could refuse to allow a work to be published or permit it only under strict conditions (including royalties!!).

**141 Are there any works that may be subject to publication right now?**

Possibly. It is arguable that works that existed before they were covered by legislation, and which have never been published, might never have been in copyright and therefore could be eligible for this new right, which applies only to works in which copyright has expired.

## Making available right

### 142   When does making available right apply?

This does not apply to literary, dramatic or musical works - only the performances of them (see paragraph 687).

## Duration of copyright in literary, dramatic and musical works

### 143   Does copyright last for the same period for all literary, dramatic and musical works?

No. There are different periods of copyright as described below.

## Published works

### 144   What constitutes 'published'?

Published means issuing copies to the public. This in turn means putting into circulation copies not previously put into circulation. Note that the emphasis is on copies. Making a single copy does not of itself constitute publication. The definition also includes making the work available through an electronic retrieval system.

### 145   How long does copyright last for published literary, dramatic and musical works?

This depends on the country of origin of the work. If the work was published in an EEA country (see the next paragraph for the definition of EEA) or the author is an EEA national, then the copyright in published literary, dramatic or musical works lasts for 70 years from the end of the calendar year in which the author dies. Copyright always expires on 31 December, never in the middle of a year.

*Example*: Author died on 5 January 1902. Copyright expires on 31 December 1972. Author died on 29 December 1902. Copyright still expires on 31 December 1972.

## 146   What is the EEA?

It is the European Economic Area, which comprises (as at June 2004): Austria, Belgium, Cyprus, Czech Republic, Denmark, Estonia, Finland, France, Germany, Greece, Hungary, Iceland, Ireland, Italy, Latvia, Liechtenstein, Lithuania, Luxembourg, Malta, Netherlands, Norway, Poland, Portugal, Slovakia, Slovenia, Spain, Sweden and United Kingdom.

## 147   What about works published outside the EEA?

These are protected for the same length of time as they would be in their own country if none of the authors are EEA nationals. If a work is published in a country that gives only 50 years protection then that is all it will get within the EEA.

## 148   Supposing a work was published simultaneously in several countries both within and outside the EEA?

In this case, it is considered as an EEA publication. Note that 'simultaneous' means within 30 days of first publication. So a work could be published in, say, Australia one day but, provided it was also published in an EEA country within 30 days of that first publication, it would still qualify for EEA protection.

## 149   Supposing the work is anonymous or has no personal author?

Anonymous works first published within the EEA, which include works that have no personal author such as annual reports of organizations, or anything with no identifiable personal author, remain in copyright for 70 years from the end of the year in which they are created. If they are published during that period then the 70 year period starts all over again. Otherwise the work is protected for the length of time it would have been published in the country of origin (usually 50 years).

### 150 Supposing the author died before the work was published – does this make a difference?

If the work was published after the author died but before 1 January 1969 then copyright expires 50 years from the end of the year in which the work was published. If the author died on or after 1 January 1969 then the 70 year rule applies as in other cases, but see paragraph 147 for non-EEA authors.)

## Compilations and periodicals

### 151 What about works made up of contributions by several people?

The copyright expires separately for each contribution. So the copyright in papers in a conference proceedings all expire at different times, depending when each contributor dies. However, the copyright in the typography will expire 25 years after the end of publication (see paragraph 168 on typographical arrangement).

### 152 When does the copyright in a periodical issue run out?

The copyright in each article will run out 70 years after the death of the author (as for any other published literary work) but the copyright in the periodical issue as a whole (the typography) will expire 25 years after publication. If the periodical was published outside the EEA and none of the authors is an EEA national, then copyright lasts for only as long as the country of publication provides.

### 153 Supposing the work contains illustrations by someone other than the author?

The copyright in the text and in the illustrations is quite separate. For example, the copyright in the drawings accompanying A. A. Milne's *Pooh Bear* stories will last much longer than the stories themselves.

## Unpublished works

### 154 What if the work is unpublished?

The situation may sound complicated. If the author died before 1 January 1969, was a national of an EEA state and the work was unpublished at that time, copyright expires on 31 December 2039. If the author died on or after 1 January 1969 the work is protected for 70 years from the end of the year in which the author dies. If the author is not a national of an EEA state then copyright expires at the end of the term of protection given by the author's national laws.

*Example*: Author died on 22 November 1955. Copyright expires on 31 December 2039. Author dies on 3 December 1990. Copyright expires on 31 December 2060 (death + 70 years).

### 155 What if the author is still alive?

Copyright will last until 70 years after the end of the year in which the author dies, just like a published work or, if from outside the EEA, the length of time the author's own nation gives.

### 156 Does this mean that all unpublished works cannot be used by anyone until 2039?

No. If the work was held by the library or archive before 1 August 1989 and the author was already dead, then these documents can be copied, even with a view to publication, provided that the author has been dead for 50 years if the document is 100 years old. Note that copying is allowed 'with a view to publication' – the library or archive does not authorize publication; clearance for this must be arranged by the prospective publisher.

*Example*: An author wrote a poem in 1875 and died in 1910. The poem could be copied after 31 December 1975. Note, however, that 'view to publication' does not mean they can be published – only copied in preparation for plans to seek permission to publish.

**157  What about anonymous and pseudonymous works?**
Unpublished anonymous or pseudonymous works are protected for 70 years from the end of the year in which they are created or 70 years from being first made available to the public. However, where a work was created before 1 August 1989 copyright protection must last until 2039, regardless of the assumed date of creation. Despite this, if it is reasonable to assume the author has been dead for 50 years, then the work can be treated as out of copyright.

**158  What happens once anonymous or pseudonymous works are published?**
They are protected for 70 years from the end of the year in which they were published. This includes not only publishing, but public performance or broadcasting.

**159  Supposing it is not possible to judge when a document was created?**
There are special provisions for this situation. Where it is not possible by reasonable enquiry to find the identity of the author and it is reasonable to suppose the copyright has expired, then the work may be treated as out of copyright.

**160  What constitutes 'reasonable'?**
This is not defined. Common sense and professional judgement are needed to make a guesstimate as to when a work might have been written. One learned judge said that 'what is reasonable is what seems reasonable to the man on the Clapham omnibus'.

### 161   How is the length of copyright worked out if there are several authors?

Where a work has joint authorship, copyright lasts until 70 years after the end of the year in which the last author dies. If at least one of the authors is known, then any unknown ones are disregarded. Where some authors are EEA nationals and others are not, the work is treated as qualifying for the EEA term of protection (death + 70 years) or death of the last author to die, if this gives a longer term of protection.

*Example*: a work has three authors – two are EEA nationals and one is not. The two EEA nationals die in 1955 and 1960, respectively, giving a term of protection until 2030, but the third, non-EEA author, whose country gives 50 years protection, does not die until 1995, giving protection until 2045.

### 162   How long does Crown Copyright last?

Crown Copyright in a literary, dramatic or musical work lasts for 125 years from the year in which the work was created or 50 years from the year in which it was first commercially published, provided this happens within 75 years of the year of creation. In other words, 125 years is the maximum.

*Example*: A report is prepared in 1930. Its copyright will run out in 2055. But if it is published commercially, say, in 1960, then the copyright runs out in 2010.

### 163   What if the author in the example did not die until 1970?

It makes no difference. Length of Crown Copyright is linked to date of creation or date of publication, not the human being responsible for creating the work.

### 164   Supposing some papers were not released because of the 'Thirty Year Rule' and were secret until then?

This makes no difference. Copyright runs from the year in which the work was created.

**165  How long does Parliamentary copyright last?**

It lasts for 50 years from the year in which the work was created.

**166  Are the publications of other governments protected in the same way?**

No. Publications of other governments are protected as if they were ordinary commercial publications in the UK. In the USA, the US Government claims no copyright in its own publications within the USA and it would seem unlikely that they should be protected in the UK in a way that they are not in the USA. So it is generally assumed that United States Government Printing Office (USGPO) publications are not protected by copyright.

**167  How long does typographical copyright last?**

Typographical copyright lasts for 25 years from the end of the year in which the work is published.

**168  So when does the copyright on a published work actually expire?**

There are two dates. One, usually the earlier, will be the typographical one, which runs out 25 years after first publication. However, the author's copyright continues until 70 (or 50) years after death. So the copyright in a book runs out in two stages. This does nothing to help people who want to copy it within that 25-year period, of course. However, it does allow republication by another publisher if the author has retained the copyright and not assigned it exclusively to the first publisher.

**169  Does this mean that every time a book is reprinted the copyright begins again?**

No. If the reprint is simply a reproduction of the original typographical arrangement, no new copyright comes into force.

**170   Supposing it is a new layout of the book?**

Then typographical copyright subsists in that particular edition.

**171   What if it is the same typesetting but a long new introduction has been written?**

There will be a new copyright in the new introduction, owned originally by the author of that introduction. The publisher can claim copyright in the whole work (introduction and text together) but the original text will only be a reproduction of an earlier text and is covered only for the time that typographical copyright lasts.

*Example*: Shakespeare is long out of copyright but a new edition of his works will go into copyright for 25 years to protect the typography. This does not stop someone else bringing out their own edition or photocopying older editions that are out of copyright.

**172   Can any copying at all be carried out without permission?**

The law makes certain exceptions to the exclusive rights that owners enjoy over their works. The most important for libraries, archives and information providers are certain rights to copy and lend copyright works.

**173   For what purposes can a copyright work be used without the owner's consent?**

Three reasons are listed. The most commonly claimed and most frequently quoted is fair dealing (see below).

# Exceptions

## Fair dealing

**174   What is fair dealing?**

Fair dealing is a concept, which has never been defined. What it seems to be saying is that there may be good reasons for copying something so long as the copying does not harm the copyright owner but nevertheless benefits either the individual or society generally.

**175   Does fair dealing apply to all copyright works?**

Yes, but the different types of fair dealing apply differently to different classes of material. It applies to literary, dramatic, musical or artistic works for research and private study but not to audio-visual materials such as broadcasts, film, video or sound recordings, although these materials are covered by fair dealing for news reporting and criticism and review.

**176   How much of a work can be copied under fair dealing?**

Nobody knows for certain – it is a matter of individual judgement in each case. What is clear is that until a substantial part of a work is copied there can be no infringement, so such defences as fair dealing are not needed. But see Section 9 for when a work is also a database.

**177   What is a substantial part?**

See paragraph 51.

**178   So is there no guidance at all?**

In the law, no. Various guidelines have been issued in the past but they are guidelines only. The British Copyright Council has issued a set of guidelines, outlining what it thinks is fair from an owner's viewpoint. Other organizations such as Ordnance Survey, the British Standards Institution and Goad Publishing issue guidelines too, but see Section 10.

**179   How can anyone judge if copying something is 'fair'?**

Look at the amount to be copied in conjunction with the reason for making the copy. No concrete examples can be given but consider the following situations. A student wishes to photocopy a five-verse poem from a collection to study at home; a researcher wishes to publish four out of its five verses in a commercially published criticism of the poet. One is research and private study, the other criticism, both of which are justifications for claiming fair dealing. But the first would seem more likely to be 'fair' than the second. Copying a whole work, which has long been out of print and unavailable, might be 'fair', but copying the same work just to save buying a copy is obviously not. Now that the new legislation is in place, research must be for a non-commercial purpose.

## 180   What are the justifications for fair dealing?

The law recognizes several. The one most commonly cited in libraries is copying for research or private study. The other purposes are criticism and review, and reporting current events.

## Research for a non-commercial purpose

## 181   What constitutes 'research'?

The word is not defined in law but the court would probably give it its natural meaning.

## 182   What does 'non-commercial' mean?

The law does not say and it must be up to each individual to decide if the copying is fair and for a non-commercial purpose. The Patent Office has some general guidance on its website (www.intellectual-rproperty.gov.uk) but lists of suggested possible commercial and non-commercial uses, together with areas of uncertainty, are listed in Appendix 3.

## 183   Are there any other restrictions?

Yes. When copying something for non-commercial research purposes the source must be acknowledged.

## 184   What can be done for someone who does want a copy for commercial purposes?

The copying must be done with the permission of the copyright owner. Usually this is done through a licence offered by the appropriate licensing agency (see Section 10), but if none of the licences mentioned there apply, then permission must be sought directly from the copyright owner. This may be the author or the publisher depending on the circumstances.

### 185   Is private study limited to students?

Not at all, if, by 'student' is meant someone in an academic institution. Anyone undertaking training or education of any kind, including leisure courses such as evening classes in hobbies or holiday languages, can reasonably claim fair dealing as a 'student'. But to do this the copying must be done by the student personally and not on behalf of the student.

### 186   Can this be done by someone in industry and commerce?

This would be difficult to justify as the definition of private study now specifically excludes 'any study which is directly or indirectly for a commercial purpose'. So, once again, the user will need to make this judgement for each copy made for private study purposes.

### 187   Why private study?

Private study is thought of as being done alone. Therefore multiple copying for classroom use cannot be private study and is provided for separately under educational copying (see paragraph 208 and following).

### 188   Does fair dealing allow the making of more than one copy?

If the student or researcher does the copying themselves it might be possible to make more than one copy.

*Example*: Suppose a student has to go on a geography field trip. Two copies of a small portion of a map may be needed – one for use in the field (where it may get muddy or torn) and the other for the file relating to the project. If two copies are made they must be for the personal use only of the person who made them.

### 189 Supposing the student wants a copy for personal use and one for a friend?

Not allowed! If any copying is done on behalf of someone else then the person making the copy must not make it if they know that this will result in a copy of substantially the same material being supplied to more than one person at substantially the same time and for substantially the same purpose. But always remember that your institution may have a licence, which would allow this.

*Example*: Three students may make for themselves one copy each of, say, a journal article, for use in a lecture or project. But if one makes copies for personal use and copies for the two friends then this is an infringement.

### 190 What do all these 'substantiallys' mean?

They are not defined but it would seem likely that someone copying pages 9–14 for themselves and 10–16 for a friend or colleague would have copied 'substantially the same material' and that this copying, if done on Monday and Wednesday of the same week for use in the same tutorial or related experiments at the laboratory bench, would constitute at substantially the same time and for substantially the same purpose.

### 191 What about coin-operated machines then?

Although these are not dealt with specifically, the Act differentiates between copies made by students or researchers themselves and those made for them by other people. Although nothing is said in this context about providing equipment that might be used for infringing purposes, it is clear from another part of the Act that it is not an offence to possess equipment that can be used for breach of copyright, as opposed to equipment that can be used only for breach of copyright. It would be foolish for any librarian deliberately to turn a blind eye to copying that was beyond the law and a suitable notice giving details of what is and is not allowed should be displayed (contact CILIP for a suggested text), but whether a librarian could actually be held responsible is open to doubt. Any notice should refer to the new Copyright Act and its restrictions. These should also be mentioned in any publicity for the library's services and any user education courses that are offered. Generally librarians are expected to use their best endeavours to ensure that machines in their care are not used for infringements of copyright.

## 192   What if the person asks the librarian to do the copying for them?

What the law says, in a rather roundabout way, is that copying by libraries is only fair dealing if the special conditions about copying by libraries are observed. If the library steps outside these conditions then the copying is not fair dealing and becomes an infringement. Copying by libraries is dealt with in detail in paragraph 224 and following.

## 193   What about downloading from databases?

See Section 9 for detailed guidance.

## 194   What about databases stored on CD-ROM?

Again, see Section 9.

## 195   What about copying from collections of data such as telephone directories?

Such items as telephone directories and timetables are now classed as databases. See Section 9.

## 196   What about things like Yellow Pages?

In the specific case of *Yellow Pages* BT has said that it considers one page or one classified section, whichever is the smaller, to be a reasonable amount to copy.

## Criticism or review

### 197   What is criticism or review?

Criticism or review is important for all kinds of librarians. It is allowed to quote parts of a work when writing critical essays or reviews such as book reviews in *Update* or comparisons of different authors' works in academic research.

### 198   How much can be quoted?

Again, it is not stated but the publishers used to say that they felt a single extract of up to 400 words or a series of extracts (none of which was over 300 words) totalling not more than 800 words was not unfair. For poems this was given as 40 lines or not more than 25% of the whole poem. These figures are quotes simply to indicate some thinking on the quantities that might be involved. The source of the quotations must be given, for example the full bibliographic reference in a review is essential as the reviewer may be encouraging the reader to buy a copy! The same is true if a criticism is being written of the writings of a single author. Libraries that prepare their own reviews for the general public or in the form of information bulletins for researchers should note the conditions under which, and to what extent they can quote the works mentioned.

### 199   Are there any rules to be observed?

Yes. The work quoted must have been made available to the public and the source of the quotation must be acknowledged.

### 200   What does 'made available to the public mean'?

In this context it includes:

- the issue of copies to the public
- making the work available by means of an electronic retrieval system
- rental or lending of copies of the work to the public

- performance, exhibition, playing or showing of the work in public
- communication to the public of the work by electronic means.

**201 Does this review idea extend to news bulletins?**

No. Reporting current events is a separate justification for claiming fair dealing. The production of news bulletins, current events information and similar news items can use any news material provided that sufficient acknowledgement of the source is made. Such activities as news clippings services, circulated to staff, are justified on these grounds but each clipping must have the source noted on it. Fair dealing in this context does not extend to photographs. (See also paragraph 435.)

## Reporting current events

**202 What is a current event?**

A current event is something defined less by time than by current interest. It can be something that happened yesterday or today, but, equally, it might be something that happened several years ago but which has a bearing on events happening now.

**203 Can any material be used?**

Any work can be used except a photograph.

**204 Supposing the news items that are needed include a photograph?**

Clearly the law is intended to protect the very considerable investment in photography made by newspapers and without this exception any evening paper could use the photographs of any morning paper for its news story. In theory this applies to internal and local news bulletins made from clippings but it is very difficult to exclude a photograph in the middle of a piece of news text. Technically it should be blacked out but this is often done in the photocopying process anyway! The alternative is to retype the necessary text. But note that licences are now available for copying some newspapers through the Newspaper Licensing Agency (NLA). Note that the NLA has a limited repertoire as far as literary works are concerned but a wider one for typographical arrangement. This may limit its ability to license some materials. This does not stop you reformatting the actual contents in some way for re-use. See Section 10.

### 205 Supposing the news bulletin is prepared and displayed electronically?

The same rules apply as for a clippings service.

### 206 Are there any other restrictions?

Yes, the source of the work quoted must be acknowledged unless this is not possible for reasons of practicality or otherwise.

### 207 What does that mean?

I suppose it means you must acknowledge the source if you can find it out.

## Educational copying

See also Section 10.

### 208 Are the amounts allowed to be copied for educational copying just as vague as in fair dealing?

No, the rules are quite different.

### 209 What is the difference between copying for educational purposes and copying for private study?

Private study does not mean for classroom use. Educational copying can be for classroom use. All librarians in any organization where teaching takes place should be aware of what is allowed, as the materials in their care are frequently used for educational purposes. This is also true for public libraries, which are used for project work. Educational copying exceptions do not apply to training in commercial or industrial companies.

## 210   Can a teacher or pupil copy anything for use in the classroom?

A teacher or pupil may copy out all or part of a copyright work in the course of instruction (such as a poem) onto the black-board or into an exercise book for the purposes of instruction, but they may not copy it using a reprographic process, for instance by photocopying.

## 211   Does instruction apply only to schools and universities?

No. Instruction can take place in industrial or commercial train-ing courses, military camps or anywhere else. Note that 'instruc-tion' is not the same thing as 'education' for copyright purposes.

## 212   Can any amount be copied?

If the work is unpublished then any amount can be copied. If it is published then the copying must be fair. In other words, so much of a work must not be copied that it becomes unnecessary to buy a copy or copies of the work for teaching purposes or it is done to avoid being copied under the CLA licence.

## 213   Are there any other restrictions?

Yes, the source of the work must be acknowledged.

## 214   What about copying for examinations?

Anything can be copied for the purposes of setting the questions or providing the answers, except musical works, which may not be photocopied to allow the pupil to perform the work. A further problem is determining when continuously assessed work counts as part of an examination and when it is classroom teaching.

**215 Does 'anything' really mean anything?**

Yes, except for musical scores as mentioned above.

**216 What if a student needs to include some copyright material in a thesis for a degree?**

This would seem to be covered in providing the answers to an examination. There could be problems if the thesis is subsequently copied for other purposes or published.

**217 What happens if several children come into the public library, all asking for copies of the same thing for their project?**

Only one copy can be provided. It is unclear at what age a child could sign the necessary declaration form (see paragraph 257) as a legal minor. However, although schools operated by local authorities usually have a licence to copy necessary materials, such licences may allow copying only from books and magazines in the school's own collection and not those held by other libraries. Teachers should check with the CLA or NLA terms as appropriate.

**218 Are there any restrictions?**

Yes, the source of the material quoted in the question must be acknowledged but students do not have to acknowledge the source when answering them. But it would be a poor answer that contained unacknowledged quotes!

**219 What about including some copyright material in collections put together by teachers?**

There are special rules governing this that should be known by the teacher or publisher and not worry the librarian too much. Section 33 of the Act sets out the limits for this sort of publishing, for which librarians are sometimes asked to provide the original material to copy.

## Copying for educational establishments

**220   What counts as an educational establishment?**
An educational establishment is defined as:

- any school
- any university allowed to award degrees under Act of Parliament or Royal Charter
- any institution empowered to offer further or higher education under the Education (Scotland) Act 1980, the Education and Libraries (Northern Ireland) Order 1986 or the Education Reform Act 1988. (See SI 98/1068 for exact details.)
- any theological college.

**221   Can anyone else exercise these privileges?**
Yes, any organization, provided the education is for a non-commercial purpose.

**222   Multiple copying is not allowed and fair dealing does not extend to classroom copying, so what can be done for teachers who need multiple copies of parts of works for use in instruction. Surely they do not have to rely on writing everything out by hand?**
No! The Act allows one of two ways forward. If a licence is obtainable to cover the needed materials, then that licence should be taken out and adhered to. All local authorities and many universities have taken out such a licence and the first thing is to check what it covers and what it allows. If no licence is obtainable then the law allows that up to 1% of a work may be copied for classroom use in any three-month period specified by the Act. (The Act actually lays down that these periods are fixed as 1 January to 31 March, 1 April to 30 June, 1 July to 30 September and 1 October to 31 December.) These allowances may not be claimed if the person doing the copying knew, or ought to have known, that a licensing scheme was available but

no licensing scheme is allowed to restrict copying to below these very small limits.

**223    Can the library do this copying on behalf of the teacher or lecturer?**
Yes. But make sure the terms of the licence are known before agreeing to do such copying.

## Libraries and archives

### Copying published literary, dramatic or musical works

**224    Are there exceptions for libraries?**
This is the most important limitation on owners' rights as far as librarians and archivists are concerned. The main user group mentioned in the Act is libraries and archives. The special exceptions for libraries and archives apply to literary, dramatic and musical works but not to artistic works. There are no special exceptions for museums (other than copying unpublished works, see paragraph 338 and following). These privileges are often referred to as library privilege. This is a useful shorthand term but is not a legal one. Note that these rules apply where the librarian or archivist makes the copies on behalf of the user. Where users copy for themselves they claim fair dealing and not library privilege.

**225    Are the terms 'library' and 'archive' defined?**
No. There are definitions of prescribed libraries and archives but not of libraries and archives generally.

**226    Are the terms interchangeable?**
No. Specific allowances are given to libraries and archives separately.

**227 So what are libraries allowed to do that is special?**

Quite a lot. First, they can supply copies of works to their users.

## Copying for users - periodicals

**228 What constitutes a periodical?**

This is not defined. The word 'periodical' implies some concept of being issued at periods of time. Therefore monographs in series, technical report literature and publishers' series would probably not count as periodicals as they are not linked to any timescale. A further problem could be newspapers. Although most librarians view newspapers as periodicals some dictionaries define the word 'periodical' as excluding newspapers!

**229 Is there a limit on how much of a work can be copied for a user?**

Yes. There are different limits for different kinds of material. In the case of a periodical, no user can be supplied with a copy of more than one article in the same periodical issue.

**230 Can the user have more than one copy of the same article?**

Not under any circumstances.

**231 Supposing the volume of separate issues has been bound, how does this affect copying?**

The law is not specific but it seems likely that the interpretation would be that not more than one article could be copied from any one original periodical part as issued to the public. The subsequent binding by the library would, in any case, reduce the freedom to copy for the user, if this view were taken, as the bound volume would become the 'issue'. As this would change the amount allowed to be copied by an action beyond either the copyright owner's or the user's control, it is unlikely that this view would be taken. The original form of publication is therefore what really counts.

**232  Supposing the article includes some drawings or photographs. Is it allowed to copy these as well?**

Yes. If an article is copied for someone, then it is allowed to copy any accompanying illustrations. 'Accompanying' is an important word. If the article is in, say, an art journal and is supplemented by high-quality plates of paintings just to further illustrate the artist's work, these may not be copied unless they are intrinsic to the understanding of the text.

**233  What counts as an 'article'?**

Unfortunately this term is only defined in very general terms. An article, in the context of an article in a periodical, means an item of any description.

**234  Does this include things like advertisements, the title page, contents page or index?**

Yes, so the user should not really be supplied with an article from an issue and also the contents page.

**235  What about making copies of contents pages and circulating them for information among staff?**

This is not allowed. In the first place, it is multiple copying and secondly the library cannot make copies for people unless they sign the declaration form first.

**236  So is copying title pages not allowed at all?**

It would be possible to circulate one copy of the contents page among staff, provided one of them asked for the copy in the first place. Alternatively, it is a good idea to write to the publishers concerned and ask if they will permit this. Most say they will as it is good advertising for their journals, but some take the view that it could encourage related copying (more than one copy requested by different people at the same time for the same purpose). See also paragraph 268 and following.

### 237   Supposing the user wants two articles from the same issue?

Only one can be provided. However, it might be possible for the user to claim fair dealing if he or she borrowed the periodical issue and made the copies personally. This would then require a fair dealing defence so the copying should not be of such an extent that this was not a plausible argument.

### 238   If a publisher charges a higher rate for a library subscription to a periodical, can more copying be done?

No, unless the publisher has specifically stated this in the publicity, catalogues or in a specific letter to the library.

### 239   Can articles be copied from newspapers?

Yes. Whether the rules for copying from monographs or periodicals apply is slightly doubtful. Note also there is a Newspaper Licensing Agency (see Section 10).

### 240   But to copy one article from a newspaper often involves incidentally copying another, or at least part of another. What is the position then?

Technically only the article actually required can be copied. To be perfectly correct all other parts of the page should be blanked out! But this would be incidental copying, really, copying as an accident or done simply in the normal process of doing what is allowed. If a case were brought, it might be possible to argue, by analogy, incidental copying similar to that allowed for artistic works in photographs (see paragraph 402) but that is only an opinion.

### 241   Does the copying of articles extend to conference proceedings?

It depends on the nature of the conference publication. Many annual or more frequent conferences appear simply as 'Proceedings of the xth conference on . . .' and could be viewed as a serial. Others with no clear numbering, or with monographic titles, must be treated as books. If the conference is held regularly then it could be a periodical (annual is the most common frequency). Conferences that are merely numbered with no indication of the timescale in which they are held will most likely be monographs (non-periodical publications).

**242   What about technical reports in a numbered series?**
Generally these must be treated as separate monographs.

**243   Suppose the periodical issue consists of just one article?**
The law specifically states that one article may be copied from a periodical issue. It seems clear that this allows the copying of an article if it constitutes the entire issue of a periodical although any other material in that issue, such as title page, advertisements or other ephemeral material, must not be copied.

**244   What about individually tailored information services?**
The arrangement whereby the librarian scans various information services for material that is considered relevant to the researches of library users and then obtains copies of these items and passes them on to users without being asked for them is an infringement.

**245   What can be done for researchers in this situation?**
There is no reason why a librarian may not produce a current awareness bulletin from which staff select and request items they require, but they must ask for items, not have them sent gratuitously.

**246   Suppose they are two students at a university requiring the copies for totally different courses?**
This does not seem to matter. They still require them for sub-

stantially the same purpose and they are receiving instruction in the same place although this might not apply if two lecturers asked for the same material for totally different courses.

## Abstracts

**247  Does the abstract that goes with a journal article have a separate copyright?**

Yes. It is a distinct work, which can stand alone – otherwise it is not really an abstract.

**248  Can any abstract be copied?**

Yes, but not those that appear in abstracting services such as *Chemical Abstracts.* The law says abstracts that accompany articles in scientific or technical journals come into this exception but just what 'scientific' or 'technical' means is open for discussion.

**249  Can the abstract be copied with the article?**

Yes. The law states that such abstracts can be copied freely unless there is a licensing scheme that covers them, in which case you must belong to the scheme to copy the abstracts. At the time of writing no such scheme has been devised.

**250  How about writing abstracts for information services?**

It is quite in order to prepare abstracts from scratch by summarizing the article concerned using skill and knowledge to read the article and present the information in a different form. You should not use actual text from the original article. Once written, the copyright belongs to you or your employer as appropriate.

**251  Can they be used in information bulletins?**

Yes. They can be duplicated, printed, given away or sold, either freely or by licence.

## Monographs

**252 What is the definition of monograph?**

The law does not use the word 'monograph' (or 'book' except in relation to Public Lending Right), but rather 'published edition other than an article in a periodical'.

**253 Can librarians copy books (monographs)?**

The librarian may supply one copy of not more than a reasonable proportion of a book to a reader.

**254 What constitutes a 'reasonable' proportion?**

This is not defined but the British Copyright Council has indicated that it views '10% or a chapter' as reasonable. Although this is not a legal definition it is a helpful guideline. It seems safe to assume that a reasonable proportion is larger than a substantial part because if less than a substantial part had been copied, there would be no need to claim any defence. Like substantial part and fair dealing this is a matter of individual judgement.

**255 Supposing a book consists mostly of photographs and plates?**

Each item will be a copyright item in its own right and must be treated as such. Libraries may not copy artistic works (such as photographs and plates) on behalf of users unless they accompany the text requested. So the library may copy illustrations accompanying material but the illustrations must accompany the text. Text that accompanies illustrations will not count for this allowance.

## Restrictions on copying for users

**256 Can any librarian copy for someone under these conditions?**

Yes. There is no discrimination in favour of prescribed libraries in this area. But the copying must be for research for a non-commercial purpose.

### 257   Are there other restrictions?

Yes. The librarian can copy an article from a periodical or part of a published work only if the user signs a declaration form. The form must state that:

- a copy has not previously been supplied
- the copy will not be used except for research for a non-commercial purpose or private study and that a copy will not be supplied to any other person
- to the best of [the user's] knowledge no person with whom [the user] works or studies has made or intends to make at about the same time a request for substantially the same material for substantially the same purpose
- if the declaration is false the copy becomes an infringing copy and the reader is responsible as if [the user] had personally made the copy.

In addition, the user is required to pay a sum, which will cover not only the cost of copying but make a general contribution towards the running of the library.

### 258   Those 'substantiallys' have turned up again. Are they defined in this part of the Act any better than in the other?

In a word, no. The same uncertainty applies (see paragraph 51).

### 259   Can a user really be expected to sign a statement about the intentions of other people?

No, that is not what is being asked. Users sign to say that to the best of their knowledge nobody else is going to ask for copies of substantially the same material . . . . Thus the user can be in complete ignorance and truthfully sign the form.

## 260    Does this declaration have to be made when the request is made?

No. But it must be made before the copy is handed over. These two actions often coincide in smaller libraries but in large libraries or public libraries there can be a waiting time between the request and the arrival of the copy. It is perfectly in order to obtain the signed declaration at the time the request is made but it must be borne in mind that in some circumstances a copy may not be supplied but the original lent instead. In this case the declaration is superfluous. On the other hand the requester may not be aware that the request will be fulfilled by a photocopy so it would be reasonable not to ask for a signature until the document was handed over.

## 261    What happens when requests are received by telephone or letter?

It may be possible that the request can be processed but the copies cannot be handed over until the declaration form has been signed. This may well cause rather long correspondence but there is no easy way round this.

## 262    Can the declaration be sent by fax?

It seems likely. Fax is widely regarded in legal circles as an adequate substitute for the actual signed document. Much larger transactions than library photocopies are settled in this way!

## 263    Can the declaration be made electronically rather than having to visit the library in person?

Although the Electronic Communications Act allows electronic signatures for all kinds of transactions, where legislation specifically requires a physical signature, this must be repealed. As at April 2001 this has not happened for this provision in the copyright law.

**264   Must payment be made before the copies are handed over?**

No, but payment must be made at some point. (See paragraph 289.)

**265   What if the person making the request lives overseas?**

This makes no difference. Even though the amounts may be small, payment cannot be avoided.

**266   What if something is required urgently?**

You need to use ingenuity but the law must be observed.

**267   Is there a standard form in which this declaration must be made?**

Yes. The text is published in Statutory Instrument 89/1212 Schedule 2 Form A (as amended in 2003) and also in Appendix 4 at the end of this book.

So, as long as these conditions are met, can any librarian copy for a user?

It is not so simple. The user must sign a declaration but, in addition, the librarian must be satisfied that the requirements of two or more people are not similar or related and that no person is furnished with:

- more than one copy
- more than one article from a periodical issue or more than a reasonable part of any other published work.

**268   How can a librarian tell if the requirements of two or more users are 'similar'?**

Similar is defined only in terms of substantially the same material at substantially the same time and for substantially the same purpose!

**269    So is there really no guidance as to what these terms mean?**

No. It is fairly easy to give examples of what would be regarded as substantial as in paragraph 51, but it is very difficult to say what would not be regarded as substantial in these terms.

**270    How can a librarian tell if requirements are related?**

This is a lot easier. Related is defined as 'those persons receiving instruction to which material is relevant at the same time and place'. This is to stop classroom copying by libraries in educational establishments.

**271    Can the librarian rely on the user's honesty when signing the declaration form?**

Basically, yes, in respect of the purposes for which the copy is required, but certain measures to ensure the law is complied with must also be in place.

**272    Supposing the user signs the declaration and it turns out to be untrue?**

Librarians cannot be expected to know the inner motives of their users and the law recognizes this. The librarian may rely on a signed declaration from the reader as to the purpose for which the copy is required and the truthfulness of the statement that a copy has not been supplied by another librarian previously.

**273    Then who is liable if the user signs a false declaration?**

The law specifies that it is the user who would be guilty as if they had made the copy themselves.

**274    How can a librarian know that a copy has not been obtained from another library?**

That is not possible. But the declaration that the user signs specifically states that the user has not been supplied with a copy by you or any other librarian.

**275    Can the user give the copy to someone else?**

Perhaps. But the declaration says that the reader will not use the copy except for research or private study. Giving it away could be regarded as using it for other purposes but this is open to question. What is clear is that if the user gave it to someone else who used it for any other purpose, this would make it an infringing copy. But the reader signs a declaration to say they will not give a copy of it to anyone else – they will not give a copy of the copy with which they have been supplied to anyone else. In other words, they will not photocopy the photocopy.

**276    What happens if the user no longer requires the copy and subsequently gives these copies back to the library?**

Unless the library considers itself a prescribed library it might be wise to refuse such generosity, although another view is that the copy is perfectly legitimate and can therefore be regarded as having the status of the original and can be given to a non-prescribed library. It would be sensible to document this, just in case its status were questioned.

**277    Would it be best to destroy such copies?**

Not necessarily. The user is entitled to keep the copy and may add it to files of other papers. These are often then deposited in an appropriate department of the institution or company. A suitable registry would need to be used for depositing such material, but see the previous paragraph.

**278    If a user gives the copy to someone else, can that user have another copy from the library?**

No, because a user must sign to say they have not previously been supplied with a copy.

**279    Supposing a user genuinely lost the previous copy?**

The librarian cannot legally supply another. Readers should not be so careless! However, there seems to be nothing to stop readers borrowing the item and making a further copy for their private use. In this case, the copying would fall outside the provisions for libraries and become fair dealing.

**280  What is the position if a second user also genuinely asks for the same material as the first, equally ignorant of the request by the first person?**
If the librarian is aware of this, the second person cannot be supplied with a copy.

**281  Isn't that rather unfair on the second user?**
Perhaps so. But the idea is that a user should share the first person's copy.

**282  Do all these references to the 'librarian' really mean only the person in charge of the library?**
No. The law says that references to the librarian include a person acting on behalf of the librarian.

**283  Can any librarian make a copy for any member of the public?**
It would appear so although it might be difficult for a member of the general public to satisfy all the conditions if that person asked for a copy from the librarian of an industrial or commercial company.

**284  What about information brokers who obtain documents from libraries for their clients?**
If a broker goes to a library in person to ask for a copy to be made, and that copy is for a client, the librarian should not make the copy unless the broker can produce a signed copy of the appropriate declaration form. The broker cannot sign a declaration that the document is required by the broker personally for the purposes of research for a non-commercial purpose or private study.

**285   Could the broker be regarded as acting on behalf of the librarian?**

Not really, because the broker will actually be asking the library for the copies.

**286   Could the broker collect the properly signed forms on behalf of a client and bring them to the library to request copies?**

This would seem a possible solution but the librarian would need to be sure that the signatures on the forms were actually those of the persons requiring the copies. Signatures of agents are not allowed. However, it is unlikely that a broker would be working for someone wanting copies for a non-commercial purpose so the scenario would fail on that count if nothing else.

**287   Can the broker charge for the copies?**

No. The broker can recoup the cost through charging for other services but not for the copy itself.

**288   Must all library users pay?**

Yes. All copying done on behalf of someone else by librarians must be paid for.

**289   What is the point of making people pay?**

Basically the idea was introduced to stop publicly funded libraries being overwhelmed by demands for free photocopies. Users enjoyed a privilege but it was not to be funded from the public purse. Unfortunately the law is so framed that the rule applies to all libraries.

**290   Supposing circumstances are such that the user cannot pay?**

Legally, some way must be found for payment to be made. For example, employees in a company or researchers in a university should pay when copies are made for them. They could be reimbursed by the institution later or a voucher system could be introduced but some kind of payment should be made.

**291 Is the amount specified?**

Not directly, but it must be a sufficient amount to cover not only the cost of making the copy but also contributing towards the general running costs of the library.

**292 Is photocopying subject to VAT?**

Yes, although the amounts on individual copies may be so small that a per-page charge, which is calculated to include the VAT, is probably the most practicable way to collect this.

**293 Do users of public libraries have to pay?**

Yes. Some people have argued that the payment of local council tax is a contribution to the general expense of the library, but that would only apply to residents of the authority running the library and users must still pay for the actual cost of the photocopy.

**294 What about students?**

They should pay like everyone else although, again, it could be argued that part of their fees is for the general upkeep of the library. Again, they still have to pay for the copies.

**295 What about people in industrial and commercial companies? Can they really be expected to pay?**

Yes. Payments can be made in blocks rather than at individual times, but the library should raise an invoice to the user at regular intervals. Internal accounting procedures may allow this to be paid from a department within a company to the library, but there is no way that payment can be avoided.

## Interlibrary supply

**296 What is interlibrary supply?**

The term 'supply' has been used because it is important to distinguish between lending and copying for interlibrary purposes. For lending between libraries see paragraph 113. Copies supplied between libraries are often referred to as 'interlibrary loans' but they are actually copies supplied for retention. It is also important to distinguish between inter*library* copying, which is intended for one library to supply copies for the collection of another library, and copying for individuals who have made their request to their own library, which does not hold the material required, and which has therefore transmitted the request to another library. The law makes provision for inter*library* copying but copying by one library for users of another library must be treated as a two-stage process. See the diagram opposite if you are confused!

**297 What about supplying photocopies or microforms of works for library collections?**

This is allowed for certain libraries only.

**298 What about supplying copies through interlibrary arrangements for individual users?**

Either the library that receives the original request must send it on to another library with the declaration form (see paragraph 257) or the library that receives the request must have a clear agreement with the library to which the request is sent that the first library will collect and retain the declaration form on behalf of the second library, which made the copy. Otherwise the library making the copy has no proof that the copy was made legally.

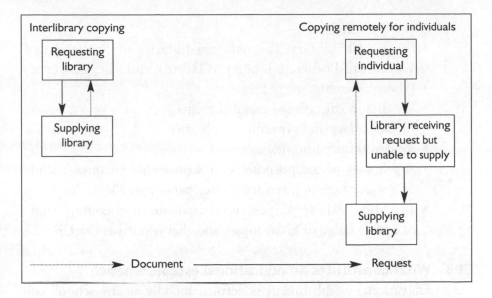

## 299   How does the British Library Document Supply Centre (BLDSC) manage to supply copies to individuals?

Exactly as described in the previous paragraph. All institutional users of BLDSC services sign just such a declaration to act on behalf of the British Library in this respect. (See also Section 10.)

## 300   Which libraries can supply copies, then?

Any library in the UK can make and supply photocopies of material in its collection.

## 301   What about receiving copies?

Only prescribed libraries may request and receive copies for their collections.

## 302   What is a prescribed library?

A prescribed library is carefully defined as any library in the following categories not conducted for profit (see paragraph 307):

- any public library that is defined as a library administered by a library authority in England and Wales; a statutory library authority in Scotland or an education and library board in

Northern Ireland
- the British Library, the national libraries of Scotland and Wales, the Bodleian Library (Oxford) and the University Library, Cambridge
- libraries in educational establishments
- Parliamentary and government libraries
- local authority libraries
- any library whose purpose is to facilitate or encourage study of a wide range of given topics (see paragraph 306)
- any library whose purpose is to facilitate or encourage study of a wide range of given topics and that is outside the UK.

### 303    What constitutes an educational establishment?

Educational establishment is defined broadly as any school, college, polytechnic or university in the public sector, but for specific details see SI 89/1068 and paragraph 220.

### 304    Is a government library restricted to those in Civil Service departments?

No, the definition includes any library conducted for or administered by an agency that is administered by a minister of the Crown. So, for example, the library of a NHS hospital would count as a government library. The library of a private hospital would not.

### 305    What is the difference between a public library and the library administered by a local authority?

This latter category is intended for those libraries that act as libraries for departments of local or county councils. For example, many planning or environmental health departments have their own libraries and some councils have a members' library for councillors' benefit.

### 306    What is this wide range of given topics just mentioned?

It is actually listed as 'bibliography, education, fine arts, history, languages, law, literature, medicine, music, philosophy, religion, sciences (including natural and social science) or technology'.

### 307 What exactly does 'conducted for profit' mean?
This is a very important phrase as it does not simply apply to the library itself but includes the organization that owns or administers the library. So the library of a major industrial company may well not be conducted for profit but the owning company certainly is, and the library is not therefore a prescribed library.

### 308 What about charities?
The library of a charity may or may not be a prescribed library, depending on the purpose of the charity. If it is a charity whose aims are primarily to facilitate or encourage the study of the range of topics stated, then the library can claim to be prescribed. If the charity is mainly concerned with other purposes such as improving social welfare, advancing human rights or promoting particular points of view, or if the charity operates commercially, then it cannot claim to be prescribed.

### 309 What about libraries of learned societies?
Many of these will qualify as the primary aim of the society will be to facilitate or encourage the study of the relevant subject. But, like charities, it will depend on the aims of the society administering the library.

### 310 What about private libraries?
Some private libraries could say they are conducted for profit and in that case they cannot qualify, but others are charitable in status and again it will depend on the nature of the charity.

### 311 Can anything be copied by prescribed libraries?
No. There are restrictions on periodical articles and books (monographs).

### 312   What are the restrictions?

First, no library may be supplied with more than one copy of any material. Secondly, no library may be supplied with a copy of more than one article from a periodical issue or even part of a non-periodical work unless the requesting library also supplies a written statement to the effect that it is a prescribed library and does not know, and has not been able by reasonable inquiry to find out, the name and address of someone entitled to authorize the making of the copy. Thirdly, the requesting library must pay.

### 313   What does 'reasonable inquiry' mean?

This is not defined but it should be remembered that, as the library that is being asked to make the copy must hold the material, it is quite possible that the requesting library could obtain the required information from the supplying library and even more likely that the supplying library could find this out anyway. However, if the material is published by a company now out of business, or in a remote corner of the world and the publisher does not reply to correspondence, then the copies can be made, but there is always the remote chance that the copyright owner might appear and challenge what has been done. Nothing is certain in the world of copyright!

### 314   Who is the person entitled to authorize the making of the copy?

As the requirement is to make a copy of all or a substantial part of the work, the publisher will probably be the only person who can authorize the making of such a copy, as publishers usually own the copyright in the total publication (as against authors who own the content of the text, illustrators who own rights in their work, and so on). However, modern publishing contracts are usually for fixed, often short, terms so many rights in individual parts of the monograph may have reverted to the author. But the publisher will still own the typographical copyright.

**315 Is a prescribed library allowed to keep the copies and add them to stock?**

Yes. This is one way that the problem of two people requiring the same material can be overcome. Reader A borrows the photocopy and returns it. Reader B then borrows it in the same way as any other library materials.

**316 What if a copy is lost or destroyed?**

A second copy could possibly be asked for as prescribed libraries may only request one copy and there is no time limit on this. However, it is a nice point that, if the photocopy had been placed in the permanent collection, then the library might be able to request a replacement at some distant date as the first photocopy is legitimate and could be regarded as part of the permanent collection. See paragraph 328.

**317 Can the library subsequently dispose of the copy to another library?**

It seems probable that this can be done only to another prescribed library that did not already have a copy of the material in question, but whether this second library would also have to pay the stipulated amount is open to question.

**318 Suppose the library sold off its collection. What should happen to the photocopies?**

They should either be sold to another prescribed library (which should pay the cost of making the copies, plus a contribution to the running expenses of the library), or be destroyed.

**319 Must libraries pay for interlibrary copying?**

Yes, but the conditions are slightly different. In this case the requesting library must pay a sum equivalent to, but not exceeding, the cost of making the copy, plus a contribution to the general running expenses of the library.

**320   Can the fees be waived?**
No. This is not allowed.

**321   Does interlibrary copying attract VAT?**
Yes, just as copying for individuals does.

**322   How can a library, which is not a prescribed library, obtain a photocopy on interlibrary loan?**
Libraries that are not prescribed libraries may not request material from other libraries for their collections but only for individuals for non-commercial purposes.

**323   What can those working in industry and commerce, and other non-prescribed libraries, do for users who want copies of documents not held in their library?**
Individuals are entitled to receive copies, provided they have signed the appropriate declaration form. They are entitled to receive copies from librarians (and any library in the UK is a prescribed library for the purposes of supplying copies), or persons acting on behalf of librarians. Therefore it would seem logical that a library user in a non-prescribed library may request a document from the librarian, who in turn requests it from another librarian, at which point the first librarian is acting on behalf of the second and supplies the copy for the use of the original user (not the librarian). Thus users can obtain a copy of a document not immediately available in their own library. An alternative is for the librarian of the prescribed library to arrange to act as an agent on behalf of the non-prescribed library to which the request will be sent for the user, but this is rather tortuous and not altogether clearly allowed. In either case the non-prescribed librarian is simply the agent (letterbox) for the prescribed library. All this is rather complex so an example might help.
*Example:* A researcher in Anybros Ltd asks the librarian of that company for a copy of an article from a periodical that Anybros

does not take, but which is taken by Sometown University. The librarian of Anybros cannot apply to Sometown University because the library of Anybros is not a prescribed library. So the librarian applies, acting simply as the letterbox for the researcher, who is entitled to ask for copies from Sometown University under the library provisions. The librarian of Anybros Ltd must be aware that Sometown University Library sees the librarian as acting as their agent to handle requests from individuals, which are to be passed to Sometown University. This would require, if not a proper agreement, at least some kind of letter of intent and the arrangement cannot be inferred from the general situation of the Copyright Act itself.

These two models are just ideas that might be allowed. There are a number of reasons why they might not, but only a test case would settle the issue one way or the other. However, the request from the researcher must stipulate that the copy is for a non-commercial purpose so this model is unlikely to be relevant in an industrial or commercial setting except in exceptional circumstances.

### 324   Can the non-prescribed library keep the copy?

This is most improbable as the copy had to be made for a non-commercial purpose and most non-prescribed libraries are functioning in a commercial context, although the law is not clear. Copies can only be requested for the use of individuals and must be handed over to them, but if they have then acquired legitimate status it may be possible to do with them anything that could be done with the original, which would include donating it to any kind of library. If this happens the actions should be clearly documented to show the non-prescribed library behaved properly.

### 325   What about brokers who request items through interlibrary loan for their clients?

The broker cannot easily do this. However, the broker could

simply be acting as a letterbox for the client as an individual, as mentioned in paragraph 286, or could enter into a proper agreement with a library to be their agent. The client would have to give assurances that the material was always for non-commercial research and would have to sign a declaration on each occasion to that effect.

### 326   Can the broker charge for the copies obtained through interlibrary loan?

No. This would be dealing in the copies, which is an infringement. The broker can, however, charge for other services and so recoup the costs necessarily incurred in obtaining the document through interlibrary loan.

## Copying for preservation

Note that for preservation purposes archives are included in the law as well as libraries.

### 327   Can libraries or archives copy their own materials for preservation purposes?

Yes, so long as the conditions stipulated are fulfilled.

### 328   Can anything in a prescribed library or archive be copied?

No. First, material has to be in the permanent collection of the library or archive. Therefore, it is not allowed to borrow a document from somewhere else, put it into the collection temporarily, copy it and then return it to the original owner. This is particularly important for collections, which are deposited for limited periods (for instance, the lifetime of the owner). Secondly, the material has to be in the permanent collection and available only for reference on the premises or for loan only to other libraries or archives. Thirdly, it must not be reasonably practicable for the librarian or archivist to purchase a copy.

**329    Is it permitted to make more than one copy for preservation?**

This seems unlikely. The Act says 'a copy' may be made.

**330    Which libraries and archives are allowed to copy for preservation purposes?**

Any prescribed library or any archive not conducted for profit and not forming part of, or administered by, an organization conducted for profit. Note that this is different for archives from the limitations on libraries, which set out specific classes of library. So the archive of a charity whose primary aim was, say, social welfare, would be a prescribed archive but the library of the same charity would not. So, the archive of a major chemical company could copy material to replace that in a university library but the reverse is not true.

**331    For exactly which reasons can material be copied for replacement?**

The law allows copying in order to replace an item in the permanent collection for reference purposes only, so that the original can be saved from constant use either by withdrawing it altogether, or relieving the amount of use made of each copy.

## Replacement copying through ILL

**332    Can library and archive materials be copied to preserve the original?**

Yes, in certain libraries and archives and under certain circumstances. The copy must be for replacing material in another library or archive that has been lost, damaged or destroyed. Clearly a library or archive cannot replace material in its own collection in this way since, if it is lost or destroyed, it is not there to copy!

**333   Can one library or archive copy for another?**

Yes, provided that the requesting library or archive provides a declaration to the effect that it is a prescribed library or archive and it has not been practicable to purchase a copy and that the copy is required as a replacement for an item in the permanent collection and for reference purposes only that has been lost, damaged or destroyed. In addition, the requesting library or archive must pay as set out in paragraph 319 and following.

**334   Which libraries and archives are allowed to copy for replacement purposes?**

First, for supplying copies for preservation and replacement, any library or archive in the UK. Secondly, for requesting and receiving copies, any prescribed library or any archive not conducted for profit and not forming part of, or administered by, an organization conducted for profit. Note that this is different for archives from the limitations on libraries, which set out specific classes of library. See also paragraph 330.

**335   Once the material has been copied, can it be used like other materials in a library or archive?**

Yes, provided that it is added to the permanent collection.

**336   So what about books or periodicals in general lending collections that are falling apart or are lost?**

These cannot qualify for copying under these special regulations. Replacement copies must be bought from the publisher, where available, or a copy obtained from another library if the conditions for that are met (the publisher cannot be traced and copy not easily purchased).

**337   Could a prescribed library or archive obtain a copy of a work from a library if the work was in the general lending collection?**

Yes, provided the copy being made was for use only in the per-

manent reference collection or in a collection available for lending to other libraries (but not individuals).

## Copying unpublished works

### 338 Can unpublished materials in a library or archive be copied for users?
Yes, under certain conditions.

### 339 What are the conditions?
First, the work has not been published before the document was
deposited. Secondly, copying may not take place if the author
has prohibited this.

*Example*: Edward Gotrip writes a novel in the hope he will
become famous and deposits the manuscript with the local public library. Subsequently it is published. The public library is
entitled to copy the manuscript (within the limits mentioned in
paragraph 254) even though the text has become a published
novel. However, Una Suming has her book published and *then*,
having become famous, deposits the manuscript with the local
public library, but no copying of it is allowed.

### 340 Can the librarian or archivist plead ignorance of the fact that the author had prohibited copying?
Not really. The law says that copies may not be made when the
author has prohibited this and the librarian or archivist knows,
or ought to know, that this is the case. Therefore, it is sensible to
keep a register of deposited unpublished material with notes on
any items that the author has prohibited the library or archive
from copying.

### 341 Can whole works be copied, or only parts?
The law allows copying of the whole of an unpublished document.

**342 Can unpublished works be copied for anyone?**

Yes, provided that the reader signs a declaration to say that the documents are required only for non-commercial research or private study, that the documents were not published before they were deposited and the reader pays a sum that covers the cost of making the copy and a contribution to the general running costs of the library or archive.

**343 Can they have more than one copy?**

No person may have more than one copy of any work.

**344 Do users have to pay?**

Yes, they must pay just as in paragraph 289.

**345 Do the restrictions on not supplying copies to more than one person for substantially the same purpose at substantially the same time apply?**

No, these restrictions are not laid down for unpublished works.

**346 Is there a standard declaration form as for published materials?**

Yes. The text is published in SI 89/1212 Schedule 2 Form B (as amended in 2003) and also in Appendix 4 at the end of this book.

**347 Can copies be supplied from one archive to another?**

No. Copying between libraries' archives applies only to published works and the sections on unpublished works allow only copying for individuals. It would seem likely, by analogy with a user of a non-prescribed library, that the user of a library or archive could ask that library or archive to apply on their behalf for a copy of an unpublished work but they would have to sign the appropriate declaration form, pay the required amount and also retain the copy for personal use, not present it to the library or archive that has acted as intermediary for them.

## Copying as a condition of export

**348   Supposing a library or archive contains material that is still in copyright but is of considerable national interest and it is decided to sell this abroad, can anything be done to copy it before it is taken out of the country?**

Sometimes, yes. If the condition of export is that a copy is made to be retained in this country it is not an infringement to make the copy or to receive it to be kept in a library or archive.

## Public administration

**349   Are there any other reasons for being allowed to copy?**

Yes. The other main reason is what the Act calls public administration.

**350   What does 'public administration' cover?**

Not as much as it would at first seem! Basically it covers:

- Parliamentary proceedings
- judicial proceedings
- Royal Commissions
- statutory inquiries.

**351   What can be copied?**

There are no limits. The Act says 'Copyright is not infringed by anything done for the purposes of Parliamentary or judicial proceedings.' The only qualification is a further allowance to the effect that if anything is copied for the proceedings and subsequently published in those proceedings this is not itself an infringement of copyright.

## Material open to public inspection

**352   Many libraries contain registers of various kinds and often act as a public information point for local authority activity such as planning applications or electoral registers. Can any of this material be copied?**

When material is open to the public as part of a statutory requirement, or is on a statutory register, any material in it that contains factual information can be copied without infringing the copyright in it as a literary work so long as this is done with the authority of the appropriate person and copies are not issued to the public.

**353   Does making a copy for a member of the public constitute 'issuing copies to the public'?**

No. Making single copies for individuals in this way is outside the definition of 'issuing copies to the public'.

**354   Can a member of the public copy an electoral register?**

Yes, and the limits are not set down legally although there may be physical or financial restraints to consider if large quantities are needed. Where whole registers are wanted it would be better for a reader to contact the local registrar.

**355   What constitutes factual information?**

Exactly that. Anything in the material that is opinion or argument for or against a case would not be covered by this allowance.

**356   Does this include maps and plans?**

No. The clause is specific that it applies to literary works only.

**357   Supposing someone wants to inspect some documents in this class but lives some way away and cannot come to consult the documents?**

Any amount of the material may be copied for such persons provided that the appropriate person gives authorization.

### 358   Who is an 'appropriate person'?

An appropriate person is the person who is required to make the material open to the public or the person maintaining the register. Such persons can authorize libraries and others to make copies as described above.

### 359   Does this apply to maps and plans as well?

Yes. There is no restriction on the type of material that may be copied for those needing it sent to them to exercise their rights. However, to prevent misuse, any maps supplied for this purpose must be marked with a statement to the effect that the maps have been supplied under the Copyright Act for the purposes of consulting publicly available material and must not be further copied without permission. The full text of this statement, which must be used as it stands, is printed in SI 89/1099. (Interestingly, the Statutory Instrument refers to statutory registers but the relevant sections of the Act do not.)

### 360   Does this also apply to statutory registers such as registers of voters?

Apparently not, because no mention is made of statutory registers in the relevant section. However, the Statutory Instrument does refer specifically to statutory registers in this section, so it is unclear just what is allowed.

### 361   Do these regulations apply only to UK materials?

Mostly, yes. The two exceptions are material made open to the public by the European Patent Office and the World Intellectual Property Organization, both intended to assist the process of patent registration.

**362   What about material which constitutes public records?**

Any material that constitutes public records under the appropriate Public Records Acts, which are open to public inspection, can be copied and copies supplied to anyone, with the authority of the appropriate officer as appointed under the relevant acts of Parliament.

**363   What if an act of Parliament actually requires that something be copied for the processes of law?**

If the copying is a required part of an act of Parliament then it is not an infringement of copyright.

**364   Supposing a copy is needed because of a national crisis such as war?**

This may then be allowed as being in the public interest. Copies were actually made for medical personnel under this clause during the Gulf War on the assumption that the Court would not permit the copyright to be defended in these circumstances.

**365   Does the existence of a separate typographical copyright prevent libraries and others from copying materials?**

No. The law specifically states that anything that can be done by way of copying with a copyright work can also be done to the typographical layout of that work.

## Visually impaired persons

**366   Supposing someone needs to use a work that is in printed form but they have a visual disability that prevents them from reading it. Can copies be made for them?**

Fortunately, new legislation came into force on 31 October 2003 to permit copies to be made for visually impaired people.

**367   Who qualifies as a visually impaired person?**

The definition is broader than might be expected. It is given as

'A visually impaired person is one who is blind or partially sighted or has uncorrectable sight-loss or who has a physical disability which makes it impossible for them hold a book or move their eyes.'

### 368 How much may be copied?

The whole of a work may be copied into a format suitable for the visually impaired person (VIP) to use.

### 369 What formats can be used?

The law does not specify or limit the formats to be used.

### 370 Are there any restrictions?

Yes, a number of limitations are put on this exception. They are as follows:

- The VIP must have lawful possession of a copy of the work or lawful access to it.
- The work must not be commercially available in the format needed.
- If the work is a musical work, transfer to an alternative format does not involve recording a performance of the work.
- The copy made must have sufficient acknowledgement of its source (bibliographic reference would seem to be implied).
- The copy must be marked to show it was made under this legislation.

### 371 What does 'lawful access' mean?

Although it is not defined, it would seem that, if the work is in a reference library to which the VIP has regular access, this would be acceptable.

### 372 Can a library or other organization charge for making the copy?

Yes, but no more than the actual cost of making it.

**373   Can one VIP pass the copy on to another?**

Yes, provided that the second person fulfils all the criteria set out in paragraph 370. But they must not copy the copy they have and pass that on instead.

**374   What if several students in a school, college or university all need copies in alternative formats?**

The copies can be made provided the institution making the copies has lawful possession of an original copy of the work. The other conditions set out for copying for individuals in paragraph 370 also apply. In addition, if the institution making the copy is an educational establishment (see paragraph 220) then they must make sure the copies are used only for educational purposes.

**375   Making these copies can be costly. Can the institution keep an electronic file so as to make copies for other students in the future?**

Yes, this is allowed with some restrictions.

**376   What are these restrictions?**

In addition to the conditions set out for individuals in paragraph 370 and for institutions in paragraph 220, the institution making the copy must:

- keep records of copies made and to whom they are supplied
- keep records of any intermediate copies lent to other institutions
- allow the copyright owner or their representative (perhaps the CLA) to have access to these records
- notify the copyright owner or representative of any copies transferred or lent to other organizations.

**377   Does this mean the copies in alternative formats can be lent?**

Yes, but only to another organization fulfilling all the criteria set out earlier.

**378 Are there any other rules?**

One important rule is that when the original is in electronic form and contains electronic management data about ownership, authorship or other information, any copies made in electronic form must also contain this data and it must not be deleted.

**379 What about licences?**

Where a licensing scheme offers the facility to make copies in alternative formats this licence must be adhered to. Also the publishing industry has issued helpful guidelines on copying for visually impaired people, which are less restrictive and cumbersome than the law. See www.pls.org.uk for more details.

**380 What is the advantage of copying under licence rather than just making the copies?**

Where multiple copies are needed the use of the licence saves a lot of bureaucratic paperwork and record keeping.

# Artistic works

## Definition

**381 What is the definition of an artistic work?**
The definition of artistic works includes:

- graphic works such as paintings, drawings, diagrams, maps, charts and plans, engravings, lithographs, etchings or wood-cuts
- sculpture
- collage
- photographs (including slides and negatives as well as microforms)
- architectural works (including buildings of any kind)
- works of artistic craftsmanship such as jewellery or pottery.

**382 Does a slide count as a photograph?**
Yes. Slides are protected in the same way as photographs.

### 383  Are overhead transparencies (OHPs) protected by copyright?

This depends on whether they contain original material prepared by the lecturer or if they are simply copies of something that already existed such as a table from a book. In the former case they might be protected by copyright if the work is original enough. Otherwise, they are another type of photograph, although when they are made on a photocopy machine it would seem equally possible to argue that they are merely photocopies on a different medium.

### 384  Do microforms qualify for copyright?

Certainly. A microfilm or microfiche ('microforms' for short) is a photograph and attracts copyright in the same way as a photograph itself. A microfilm containing several different documents may also be a database (see Section 9).

### 385  What happens if the work that has been microfilmed is still in copyright?

There are then two copyrights, one in the original document and one in the microform. To make the new copy would require the consent of the original copyright owner.

### 386  What happens if the work that has been microfilmed is out of copyright?

There is probably still copyright in the microform as a photograph even though the work photographed is out of copyright. Some authorities argue that there is no copyright in the photograph of a 'flat' object such as a document but others would argue that change of medium (from paper to photograph) requires sufficient skill to create a new original work. There is no clear-cut evidence either way and case law is inconclusive.

*Example*: A microform of *Magna Carta* would attract copyright as a photograph but the *Magna Carta* itself certainly would not.

**387 What is the situation if enlargements are made from the microform?**

The enlargements can be an infringement of microform and the original document, if the original is still in copyright, or of just the microform if that is still in copyright but the document filmed is not.

**388 Supposing a library wishes to make microform copies of works in its collection to preserve them?**

This is allowed only if the original documents are out of copyright or if they come under the special provisions for preservation (see paragraph 327 and following) .

## Authors and their rights

**389 Who counts as the author of an artistic work?**

The author of an artistic work is defined in the same terms as for a literary, dramatic or musical work (see paragraph 66). This includes, in the case of photographs, the photographer.

**390 Do authors of artistic works have moral rights?**

Yes. They are described in paragraph 25 and following. Note that authors of paintings have the right to be named as the author if the work is exhibited in public. This right has to be asserted before the exhibition takes place to be valid.

## Ownership of copyright

**391 Who owns the copyright in an artistic work?**

Ownership of the copyright of an artistic work is defined in the same terms as for a literary, dramatic or musical work (see paragraph 30 and following). The ownership of commissioned paintings, photographs or engravings made before 1 August 1989 belongs to the person commissioning the work if they actually paid for it to be done, not just paid for expenses.

**392  Who owns the copyright in a collection of slides?**

Each slide has its own copyright just like the articles in periodicals (see paragraph 42). However, there will also be a copyright in a compilation made up of slides. It may also be a database (see Section 9), depending on the way the collection is put together

**393  If a library or archive makes its own microforms, who owns the copyright?**

The copyright belongs to the library or archive. However, if the library or archive commissions an outside bureau to do the filming, ownership of the copyright will depend on the contract between the two parties. Where the microforms have been bought from a commercial company, the copyright will remain with that company, despite the status of the original documents filmed.

**394  Quite often copies of photographs supplied by libraries or archives state that, although they are old, the copyright is owned by the library or archive from whom permission must be sought to make copies or publish the photograph. Is this legal?**

The position is that the library or archive owns the photographs but not usually the copyright in them. They may well impose restrictions on the subsequent use of the photographs and that is their right as owners of the physical photographs. But they do not own the copyright in these works. If conditions are imposed, such as payment for publication, then, once these are met, the library or archive has no further claim on the photograph and certainly cannot claim the copyright in it.

## Owners' rights

**395  What rights does the owner have?**

The owner has the same rights as for literary, dramatic or musical works. See Section 3. Note that exhibiting a work is not a right the copyright owner enjoys, despite general belief to the contrary.

## Copying artistic works

### 396   What about taking photographs?

A photograph of an artistic work (say a statue or painting) is an infringement of the artist's copyright unless the work is architectural, a sculpture or a work of artistic craftsmanship and is on permanent public display in a public open space or premises open to the public.

### 397   What constitutes 'open to the public'?

This is not defined but it would certainly be a street or thoroughfare and any building to which the public had access in the normal course of events. Presumably a library, museum or art gallery is open to the public although particular parts of it may not be, so these would not count (for example, strong rooms, vaults, closed stacks, and so on). Rooms in town halls and other similar buildings are more difficult to define.

### 398   What constitutes 'permanent'?

Unfortunately this is not defined. Obviously something on loan for, say, six months, could not be permanent. Something might be on display for six months and then taken away and be counted as permanent because it was intended to be so when it was put on display in the first place.

### 399   The owners of some buildings charge copying fees to photograph artistic works housed in them even though the works must surely be out of copyright. Is this allowed?

This is not a copyright fee but a copying fee. The owners of a cathedral, for example, cannot claim there is copyright in a medieval painting but this does not stop them from charging for the privilege of having access to photograph their property. The painting is their property even though the copyright has long since expired.

## 400 What about making a slide, OHP or microform of a painting?

Photocopying, microfilming or making a transparency or slide of a drawing, engraving or painting are all infringements.

## 401 What about making a model of something in a painting?

It is also an infringement to make a three-dimensional model of a picture, photograph or painting in just the same way as photographing a statue is an infringement.

## 402 What happens if a photograph (or television programme) happens to include a piece of copyright material in the background, say an interview in front of a recent painting in a gallery?

Incidental copying of this nature is not an infringement – but it would be if the photographer or TV producer deliberately included the painting.

## 403 Supposing the library or archive holds a painting that it wishes to reproduce as a slide, poster or postcard?

If the painting is out of copyright or if the picture is of a statue or something similar on permanent public display then there is no problem. Remember, the slide, poster or postcard will attract copyright, which will be owned by the photographer or the library or archive, depending on whether the photographer was an employee of the library or archive or the library or archive simply commissioned the taking of the photograph!

## 404 Supposing there is an exhibition of children's work and the library wants to use this for publicity material or to publish it?

Technically the copyright belongs to the children individually and the permission of the child or guardian is necessary before works can be reproduced. Some teachers might argue that the copyright belongs to the school but the child is not employed there (at least not in the sense of gainful employment!) and the teacher cannot claim the copyright because the child actually did the painting.

**405    Can copies be issued to the public?**
This is restricted as for literary, dramatic and musical works. See Section 4.

## Performing the work

**406    Is it an infringement to perform an artistic work?**
There is no performing right, including the right of exhibition, for artistic works.

**407    Can the owner of a painting or other artistic work put it on public display?**
Yes. The right of display is not one of the acts restricted by copyright. Once the work has been purchased the owner of the work may display it but this does not alter the rights of the copyright owner to reproduce the work, for example on postcards, photographs or slides. But note that exhibiting an anonymous copyright artistic work, which has not been previously published or exhibited, has the effect of starting the period of copyright protection all over again to 70 years from first exhibiting the work.

## Communicating the work to the public by electronic means

**408    Supposing a television programme included a shot of a painting or sculpture. Would this be counted as broadcasting?**

Yes, unless it was incidentally included as mentioned in paragraph 402. However, if the programme were about a particular painter whose works were still in copyright then the inclusion would be deliberate and would infringe the artist's copyright. There might still be a defence of using the image for criticism or review but it would depend on the nature of the programme.

**409  Supposing the television programme is a news item about an artist who has just died and that is being reported?**

Then, to include one of the artist's paintings as part of the news might not be an infringement because this would be reporting current events (see paragraph 435).

**410  If I want to put a photograph or picture on a website, must I obtain permission from the copyright owner?**

Yes, unless it is out of copyright. Putting anything on a website is now 'communicating the work to the public by electronic means' and is an infringement of the copyright owner's rights.

## Adaptation

**411  Is there a right of adaptation in artistic works? How does it work?**

Most forms of adaptation are really copying. For example, to make a model of a painting is really an adaptation of the original to a different form as mentioned under 'models' (paragraph 401).

## Lending and rental

**412  Are artistic works subject to lending and rental restrictions?**

Yes.

**413 Does this mean that libraries may no longer lend artistic works?**

Not altogether. In the first place, this restriction applies only to material acquired on or after 1 December 1996. Secondly, lending (charging no more than operational costs) is allowed for any library except a public library.

**414 Why are public libraries excluded?**

Because the Act specifically states that public libraries, whether or not a charge is made, cannot lend these materials, except those acquired before December 1996, or under licence.

**415 Supposing there is no licensing scheme available?**

The Secretary of State has the power to implement a scheme subject to appropriate payment as determined by the Copyright Tribunal if necessary.

## Publication right

**416 Does publication right apply to artistic works?**

Yes, see paragraph 136.

## Duration of copyright

**417 How long does copyright in artistic works last?**

Although artistic works are protected in the same way as literary, dramatic or musical works there are some important differences. Some of the rules are repeated here for ease of reference. The rules about extended and revived copyright described in paragraph 43 and following also apply to artistic works.

**418 Do the rules about works originating in the EEA (see paragraph 145 and following) also apply?**

Yes the rules in this area are the same. To save unnecessary repetition the term '70 years' has been used in the following paragraphs but marked * to remind you that the EEA/non-EEA rules apply.

## Published works

### 419    How long are published artistic works protected for?

Most published artistic works are protected for 70* years from the end of the year in which the author died with the following exceptions.

## Anonymous and pseudonymous artistic works

### 420    How long are anonymous and pseudonymous works protected for?

Essentially, copyright in these works lasts 70* years from the end of the year in which they were created but, if published during that period, then 70* years from the end of the year in which they were first made available to the public.

### 421    Is 'first made available to the public' the same as 'published'?

No. In the case of artistic works it includes:

* exhibition
* included in a broadcast or cable television programme
* included in a film.

## Engravings

### 422    How long are published engravings protected for?

If published after the artist's death and before 1 January 1969, they are protected until the year of publication + 50 years. Otherwise they are protected until the year of the artist's death + 70* years.

## Unpublished works

### 423   How long are unpublished works with an author protected for?

Works of which the creator has died before 1 January 1969 and that were unpublished on 1 August 1989 are protected until 2039. All other works are protected for 70* years from the end of the year in which the author died.

## Anonymous and pseudonymous artistic works

### 424   How long are unpublished anonymous and pseudonymous works protected for?

Works created after 1 January 1969 are protected for 70* years from the end of the year in which they were created or from being first made available to the public. However, where a work was created before 1 August 1989 copyright protection must last until 2039 regardless of the assumed date of creation.

## Engravings

### 425   How long are unpublished engravings protected for?

If the engraving is unpublished and the artist died before 1 January 1969 they are protected until 31 December 2039. Otherwise they are protected from the year of the artist's death + 70* years.

## Photographs

### 426   What is the position relating to unpublished photographs?

Photographs formerly had a very complex set of rules governing expiry of copyright, but the term of protection has now been standardized at the year of the photographer's death plus 70 years or, if anonymous, 70* years from creation or, if made available to the public, 70* years from the end of the year in which that took place.

## Microforms

**427  How long is a microform protected then?**
If the author can be established, for 70* years from the year of the author's death; otherwise 70* years from the year in which the microform was made available to the public.

## Crown and Parliamentary copyright

**428  What about Crown and Parliamentary copyright?**
Where copyright in an artistic work (other than an engraving or photograph) is owned by the Crown and the work was made before 1 August 1989, copyright expires 50 years from the end of the year in which the work was created. Works made after this date are subject to the same rules as literary works (see paragraphs 145 and 162). Copyright in published engravings made before 1 August 1989 expires 50 years from the year of publication. Copyright in an unpublished engraving made before 1 August 1989 expires on 31 December 2039. However, in the case of unpublished photographs, copyright in those taken on or after 1 August 1989 will last for 125 years subject to their not being published commercially within the first 75 years; those taken on or after 1 June 1957 but before 1 August 1989 would have protection until the end of 2039; those taken before 1 June 1957 will have protection for 50 years from the end of the year in which they were taken.

## Fair dealing

**429  Are artistic works subject to fair dealing?**
Artistic works are subject to fair dealing in a similar way to literary, dramatic and musical works but there are some differences.

**430 What constitutes fair dealing in an artistic work?**

This is undefined as for other works. However, the same general rules apply (see paragraph 175 and following)

**431 Do the reasons for fair dealing – research or private study, criticism or review and reporting current events – still apply to artistic works?**

Yes. The reasons are just the same. And the restriction on research being for a non-commercial purpose applies to artistic works as well. The one area where the rules are different is reporting current events.

## Research for a non-commercial purpose

**432 How can something be copied fairly when it is an artistic work? Surely the whole of the work would be copied?**

Perhaps. Fair dealing does not exclude copying all of the work.
*Example*: An art student needs to study the different ways of portraying Hercules. The student could take photographs of modern statues, paintings and drawings for personal use to carry out the research. The photographs must not be sold or published or they would not constitute fair dealing for the purposes of research. If they were subsequently sold or published this would be an infringement as they would not be fair dealing copies and might be in direct competition with the commercial exploitation of the work by the owner such as producing postcards.

**433 What about people who go to art galleries (and libraries) and make paintings of other people's paintings?**

This would be considered as fair because it is for private study. The copy would have had sufficient original input from the copying painter to qualify for copyright protection in its own right but might still be challenged as an infringement of the copyright in the original work.

**434  Can a student include a copy of an artistic work, say, a photograph of a statue, in a thesis?**

Yes. This is for research and also providing the answer to an examination, so it is covered by educational copying. But if the thesis is published then the copyright in the artistic work is infringed.

## Private study

The rules are same as for literary works. See Section 3.

## Reporting current events

**435  Can artistic works be used to report current events?**

For general conditions see paragraph 202 but note that photographs may *not* be used for this purpose.

## Criticism or review

**436  Can artistic works be used in criticism or review?**

Artistic works may be reproduced for criticism or review provided that there is sufficient acknowledgement of their authorship.

**437  What constitutes sufficient acknowledgement?**

This is not defined but would presumably include the name of the author at least.

**438  Can an artistic work be reproduced in a journal article?**

Only if the purpose is criticism or review. Simply to include a photograph of a copyright painting to illustrate a point about modern art would not be sufficient justification.

**439  What about using a painting or photograph of a piece of sculpture to advertise an exhibition?**

This would not be allowed.

**440  What about sale catalogues that include photographs of copyright materials?**

That is allowed. There is a specific clause allowing the copying of works to advertise them for sale.

## Educational copying

**441  May artistic works be copied for educational purposes?**

Artistic works may be copied by either the teacher or the pupil themselves so long as a reprographic process is not used.

*Example*: A teacher or student could make their own copy of a map by drawing it themselves but must not photocopy it.

**442  What about examination questions?**

Anything may be done for setting questions or answering them so there are no restrictions in this area. The only requirement is that the questions acknowledge the source of the material copied.

**443  What about educational licensing schemes?**

See Section 10.

**444  What is to be done for the classroom teacher who wants multiple copies of, say, a photograph, for classroom use?**

This is not permitted. However, each student might claim fair dealing to make their own copy for research or private study purposes.

**445  Can a slide be included in, say, a film or video?**

No. That is copying just like any other form of copying.

**446  Can an OHP be made of a work for classroom use?**

Not without infringing the copyright although the publishers have indicated that they would not regard this as an infringement if a single copy from an illustration were to be made, provided the source is acknowledged.

**447 Can slides or photographs be made of artistic works for classroom use or teaching?**

Not without infringing copyright or obtaining a licence.

**448 Can copies be made of maps for classroom use?**

Photocopies for classroom use cannot be made except under the licence of the copyright owner. Teachers and pupils may copy maps out of atlases by hand or through tracing paper as this is not a reprographic process.

## Library and archive copying

See also Section 10.

**449 Can libraries and archives copy artistic works in their collections in the same way as printed materials?**

No. The special provisions for library and archive copying do not apply to artistic works at all.

**450 What is to be done for a reader who wants a copy of a photograph?**

Readers may borrow the item and copy it for themselves if they think that would be fair but the librarian is not allowed to copy on behalf of the reader. However, as fair dealing is not defined in law, it might be possible to argue that the librarian can copy for users under fair dealing provisions provided they are certain that multiple copies have not been supplied.

**451 What about copying maps for users?**

Under copyright law this is not permitted. Users may make their own copies under fair dealing arrangements. But see Section 10 on matters relating to Ordnance Survey.

**452 What about licences issued by publishers such as Ordnance Survey?**

These are really a contract between the library and the copyright owner who is allowing the library to do certain things the law does not. As owners of the copyright, Ordnance Survey (or any other publisher) is entitled to do anything it wishes with its property. Failure to observe the conditions of such a licence is a breach of contract as well as an infringement of copyright. See also Section 10.

### 453   Supposing an article in a periodical is accompanied by a photograph?

This can safely be copied as the Act makes it clear that accompanying materials can legitimately be copied, whether or not they are artistic works as such. But the photograph cannot be copied by itself – only as part of the article.

### 454   Are libraries allowed to supply copies of artistic works through interlibrary copying?

No.

### 455   What if a library or archive has lost its copy of an artistic work? Can a replacement be obtained from another library or archive?

No. Copying for preservation or replacement is restricted to literary, dramatic or musical works.

### 456   Can artistic works be copied as a condition of export?

Like literary works, an article of cultural or historical importance may be copied if a condition of the export is that a copy be made and deposited in an appropriate library or archive.

## Material open for public inspection

### 457   What is the position relating to material open for public inspection?

No specific mention is made of material open to public inspection of artistic works. For maps, however, see paragraph 359.

**458  Can artistic works be copied for public administration purposes?**

Yes, in the same way allowances apply to artistic works as to literary works.

**459  Do the rules for visually impaired people apply to artistic works?**

Yes, just like literary, dramatic or musical works. See paragraph 366 and following.

# SECTION 6

# Sound recordings

## Definition

**460 What is the definition of a sound recording?**
The definition of a sound recording is not limited in any way by format. It is any form of recording of sounds from which sounds may be reproduced. So it includes wax cylinders, vinyl discs, audio cassettes, compact discs and DVDs. It also includes sounds recorded and stored in digital form from which sounds can be reproduced.

## Authorship

**461 Who is the author of a sound recording?**
The producer.

**462 Does the producer of a sound recording enjoy moral rights?**
No (in a word!).

### 463   Who counts as the producer?

This term is defined as the 'person by whom the arrangements necessary for the making of the sound recording are made'.

## Ownership of copyright

### 464   Who owns the copyright in a sound recording?

It is owned by the record company that produced the disc. It is very important to distinguish between the copyright in the sound recording and the copyright in the material recorded.

*Examples:* A recording of a song by The Beatles will have all sorts of copyrights – the song, the music, the arrangement and the performance. In addition, there is a copyright in the actual sound recording, which is quite separate. Similarly, an interview for an oral history project will have a copyright in what the person said, which will belong to the person interviewed. There will also be a copyright in the recording made of that interview, which will be owned by the person who made the arrangements for making the recording. Again, a recording of Beethoven's Fifth Symphony will have a copyright in the recording although there is no longer any copyright in the music as such. (This is important outside libraries as the law now says it is not an infringement of the copyright in a sound recording to play it in organizations such as youth clubs. This applies only to the recording and not to the music or words of the recording.)

### 465   Who owns the copyright in an interview?

This is important for oral history and similar archives. The speaker owns the copyright in what is said but there is no copyright in the material until it has been recorded. Once it has been recorded the speaker owns the copyright in what has been said but the person making the recording owns the copyright in the sound recording as such. If the interview is transcribed then the person making the transcription may also be entitled to copyright in their transcription.

**466   Is it necessary to get permission to make such recordings for archives?**

It is advisable to obtain the permission of the speaker when the recording is made. Such permission should stipulate for what purposes the recording will be used, especially if it may be used later by a radio programme or television station. See the Oral History Society website for more information (www.oralhistory.org.uk).

## Owner's rights

**467   What rights does the copyright owner have?**

Essentially the owner has the same rights as for literary, dramatic, musical or artistic works. See Section 4.

## Copying the work

**468   Does copying include copying from one medium to another?**

Yes. To make a copy of a vinyl disc onto a tape is, of course, copying the work.

**469   Supposing the medium on which the work is stored is obsolete? Can copies be made onto a usable type of equipment?**

Not without permission or infringing copyright.

## Issuing copies to the public

**470   Who has the right to issue copies to the public?**

This is an exclusive right of the owner

## Playing the work

**471   Who has the right to play the work?**

The owner has the exclusive right to play the work.

**472 Does this mean that if a library has a collection of sound recordings, and wishes to put on a public performance of them, this is not allowed?**

This can be done either with non-copyright material (because it is too old to be protected) or with material in which the library or archive holds the copyright or if the library is covered by a Performing Rights Licence. See Section 10.

**473 Supposing the library or archive holds oral history recordings? Can these be played publicly?**

Only if the library or archive owns the copyright in both the words spoken and the sound recording itself.

**474 How can the library or archive obtain the copyright in the actual words spoken?**

This is best done by way of an agreement with the interviewee at the time of the interview. Failure to do this could lead to infringement of the speaker's copyright.

**475 If the library has a collection of sound recordings, can they be played on the library's premises?**

They can be played for private listening in carrels or somewhere similar provided that not more than one person has access to the same recording at the same time, which could be considered a public performance. Otherwise they can be played only if the library (or the library authority) has a Performing Rights Licence that covers that building. Outside these limitations, public playing of copyright material is an infringement. Check with the administration to see if the library is covered by such a licence. This also applies to films, videos, television broadcasts and radio.

## Communicating the work to the public

**476 Who has the right of communicating the work to the public?**

This is an exclusive right of the copyright owner.

**477   Presumably libraries and archives do not have to worry about restrictions on broadcasting?**

Not true. There is an increasing interest in local studies and live comments from the past, as well as folk music and recent broadcast interviews. Where this material has been prepared, recorded or given to the library or archive, it may well be in demand from local or national broadcasting stations. To allow this to be used in this way is an infringement unless the original owner gave express permission when the recording was made.

## Adaptation

**478   Who has the right of adaptation?**

This is an exclusive right of the owner

## Lending and rental

**479   As this right includes lending as well as rental, does this mean that lending services for audio materials are not allowed?**

Basically, yes. Sound recordings may not be rented to the public without the copyright owner's permission. They can be lent by other prescribed libraries (see paragraph 302) provided the fee charged only covers the cost of administration, but they cannot be lent by public libraries without a licence of some kind. See Section 10.

**480   Supposing a work is held by a library in both printed form and as, say, an audiocassette? What is the position then?**

This causes an anomaly. The printed book may be subject to Public Lending Right but the audiocassette is controlled by the licensing scheme offered by the producers of audio materials, probably through the British Phonographic Industry (BPI) licence. There are currently plans to introduce a separate licence for spoken word materials through the Spoken Word Publishers Association (SWPA). There is a further anomaly in that the money for the Public Lending Right royalty comes from the government and goes to the author; any money that may be generated by the audio licensing scheme (if there is one) is paid by the library and will probably go to the producer of the cassette.

**481  Does this mean that libraries may no longer lend records?**
Not altogether. In the first place, this restriction applies only to material acquired on or after 1 August 1989. Secondly, there are special agreements with the production industries to allow lending facilities under agreed terms. It is best to check the conditions of purchase of particular materials in the library (see also the section on licences).

**482  Why are public libraries excluded?**
Because the Copyright Act stipulates that lending by public libraries of these materials is an infringement. Furthermore, the regulations on lending and rental prohibit public libraries from lending material not covered by the Public Lending Right Scheme.

**483  Supposing there is no licensing scheme available?**
The Secretary of State has the power to implement a scheme subject to appropriate payment as determined by the Copyright Tribunal if necessary.

**484  What about the rights that performers such as singers or instrumentalists have in sound recordings?**
If it is allowed to lend the sound recording then no rights of performers are infringed by that act of lending.

## Publication right

**485   Does publication right apply to sound recordings?**
No.

## Duration of copyright

**486   How long does copyright in a sound recording last?**
Essentially 50 years from the end of the year in which it was made, but if it was published during that period or played in public or communicated to the public, then the 50 year period starts all over again.

**487   Do sound recordings have extended and revived copyright?**
No. Duration of sound recordings is not linked to a human being so the period was not extended as for some other works.

## Fair dealing

**488   Is there fair dealing in sound recordings?**
Only for very restricted purposes. See the individual headings below.

## Research for a non-commercial purpose

**489   Does fair dealing apply in sound recordings used in research for a non-commercial purpose?**
There is no fair dealing in sound recordings for the purposes of research for a non-commercial use.

## Private study

**490   Does fair dealing apply in sound recordings for the purposes of private study?**

There is no fair dealing in sound recordings for the purposes of private study.

### 491 What can be done for a student who needs a copy of a sound recording for study purposes?

There is no legal way that such a copy can be provided. The only thing to do is to obtain permission from the copyright owner.

## Reporting current events

### 492 Can sound recordings be used for reporting current events?

Yes. Short extracts from appropriate recordings can be used for new items and there is no need to acknowledge their source.

## Criticism and review

### 493 Can sound recordings be used for criticism or review?

Yes, so long as the source is acknowledged. So a broadcast that includes short extracts from sound recordings to provide comment on the work of a singer or composer is allowed.

## Library and archive copying

### 494 Can libraries and archives copy sound recordings?

No. The provisions for copying in libraries and archives are for literary, dramatic and musical works only. Remember, a 'musical work' is the score as written or printed, not a sound recording of it!

### 495 Can a library or archive copy sound recordings for preservation purposes?

Unfortunately, no. Again, these allowances are for literary, dramatic or musical works only. (But see paragraphs 713-14 on changes to legal deposit.)

**496   What can be done if a record or tape is deteriorating rapidly and will be lost if it is not copied?**

Legally, nothing if it is still in copyright. If the owner can be traced, permission can be sought but otherwise the library or archive may take a risk and produce a substitute copy. It is a matter of fine judgement whether the original copyright owner would take action if this were discovered.

**497   What happens if someone wishes to record a folksong for an archive?**

There are special rules for this. In the first place the song must be of unknown authorship and be unpublished. In other words, a real original folksong. If this really is the case then a recording can be made, so long as the performer does not prohibit this.

**498   Can the recording be kept in any local history archive?**

Not initially. Only certain designated archives can maintain collections of these items.

**499   Which archives are these?**

There are quite a number of them but they are all national in character. There is a complete list in SI 98/1012.

**500   Can copies be made from these recordings?**

Yes, provided that the archivist is satisfied that they are for research for a non-commercial purpose or private study only and not more than one copy is supplied to any one person.

**501   Is there the usual requirement that they must be paid for?**

Surprisingly, no. No mention is made of payment.

**502   Can they make copies for other archives?**

Not under copyright law. They may have other agreements with production companies which allow this.

# Other restrictions

## Educational use

**503 Is copying for educational purposes allowed?**

Only in two specific cases (and one is very specific indeed). Copying for examinations is allowed (see paragraph 214) and copying for the purposes of giving instruction in the making of films or film soundtracks is allowed provided it is done by the person giving the instruction and the purpose is non-commercial.

**504 What about using sound recordings in the classroom?**

If a sound recording is played in the classroom entirely for educational purposes and only pupils and staff are present, this is not considered a public performance and is allowed.

## Copying as a condition of export

**505 Do the special arrangements for copying materials of historic or cultural importance before export apply to sound recordings?**

Yes. If the condition of export is that a copy is made and deposited in a library or archive, then this is not an infringement and the library or archive can make the copy, or receive the copy made elsewhere.

## Material open to public inspection

**506 Do the special conditions about copying such material apply to sound recordings?**

It is not very likely that this would arise but the appropriate person may make copies either for use by persons who cannot exercise their statutory rights by consulting the material in person or if the material contains information of general scientific, technical, commercial or economic interest. Copies may not be made for persons consulting it in person.

## Public administration

**507   Can sound recordings be copied for judicial proceedings, Parliamentary proceedings and statutory inquiries, as in the case of literary works?**
Yes. There is no restriction in this case.

SECTION

# 7

# Films and videos

## Definition

**508  What is the definition of a film?**

The definition of a film includes anything from which a moving image can be produced. This covers video, videodisk, optical disc and any other new technologies that produce moving images. Despite its name a microfilm is not a film but a photograph!

## Authorship

**509  Who is the author of a film?**

The producer and the principal director. Note that it is presumed that all films have both producers and principal directors and therefore all films are treated as having joint authorship unless these two functions are performed by the same person. Note that this applies only to films made on or after 1 July 1994. Before that date the author is defined simply as 'the person responsible for making the arrangements necessary for making the film'.

### 510    Do the authors of films enjoy moral rights?

Yes, the producer and principal director both enjoy moral rights in the same way as authors of literary works. See Section 3.

## Ownership of copyright

### 511    Who owns the copyright in a film?

See Section 3 on 'ownership' for more detailed information. Ownership of many rights in a film will depend on the contracts between the various people who made the film. Remember that the film will have many copyright elements.

*Example*: A filmed interview with a song writer contains several performances of the songwriter's songs and an extract of a film containing performance of some of these songs. The songwriter may own the copyright in his or her words in the interview and the words and music of the songs; the person making the TV programme will own the copyright in the programme as a whole and the film maker will own some elements at least of the copyright in the extract of the film included in the programme.

### 512    Are the rules for 'extended' and 'revived' copyright the same?

Not quite. The extended copyright will be owned by the person who owned the copyright on 31 December 1995 but the revived copyright in the film will be owned by the principal director or his or her personal representative. But they will not own any revived copyright in the various elements of the film such as the screenplay and music and will need to negotiate with the owners of the copyright of these elements, if they are still in copyright, for rights to exploit the revived copyright in the film as a whole.

## Owners' rights

**513 What rights does the copyright owner have?**
The owner has the same rights as for literary, dramatic and musical works.

## Copying films

**514 Does this include copying from one medium to another?**
Yes, to make a copy of, say, a film to be a video is copying the work.

**515 Supposing the medium on which the work is stored is obsolete? Can copies be made onto a usable type of equipment?**
Not without the permission of the copyright owner.

## Issuing copies to the public

**516 Who has the right to issue copies of films to the public?**
This is an exclusive right of the owner.

## Showing the work

**517 Who has the right to show the work?**
The owner has the exclusive right to show the work in public.

**518** For other matters relating to performance of a work see paragraphs 65 and 93 and following, as the same basic rules apply and the same problems arise.

## Communicating the work to the public

**519 Who has the right to communicate films to the public?**
See paragraph 101.

## Adaptation

**520   Who has the right to adapt the work?**

The owner has the exclusive right to adapt the work.

## Lending and rental

**521   If this right is an exclusive right of the owner, does this mean that lending services for video materials are not allowed?**

No. Lending by prescribed libraries (other than public libraries) is allowed provided that any charges made cover no more than the administrative costs of making the loan.

**522   Does this mean that public libraries may no longer lend videos?**

Not altogether. In the first place, this restriction applies only to material acquired on or after 1 August 1989. Secondly, there may well be special agreements with the production industries to allow rental or lending facilities under agreed terms. It is best to check either the conditions of purchase of particular materials in the library or seek advice on the latest situation from CILIP (see Appendix 1).

**523   Why are public libraries excluded?**

Because public libraries may lend only materials that:

- were purchased before December 1996, or
- are covered by the Public Lending Right scheme, or
- are covered by special agreements with the industry at large, or with specific production companies or their agents.

**524   Supposing there is no lending scheme available?**

The Secretary of State has the power to implement a scheme subject to appropriate payment as determined by the Copyright Tribunal if necessary.

**525 What about the rights that performers such as singers or instrumentalists have in films or videos?**

If it is allowed to lend the film or video then no rights of performers are infringed by that act of lending.

## Publication right

**526 Are films subject to publication right?**

Yes, in the same way as literary, dramatic and musical works. See paragraph 136 and following.

## Duration of copyright

**527 Do the rules about works originating in the EEA (see paragraph 145 and following) also apply?**

Yes the rules in this area are the same. To save repetition, the 70-year rule is marked with a * to remind you that the EEA/non-EEA rules apply.

**528 How long does the copyright in a film last?**

Copyright in film lasts for 70* years from the end of the year in which the last of the following died:

- the principal director
- the author of the screenplay
- the author of the dialogue
- the composer of music specially created for and used in the film.

**529 It is not always easy to find out who all these people are or when they died. What can be done then?**

When the identity of at least one of them is known, then copyright expires as in paragraph 161.

**530    What if the identity of none of them can be found?**

Then copyright expires 70* years from the end of the year in which the film was made – unless during that time it was made available to the public.

**531    What happens if it was made available to the public?**

Then copyright runs for 70* years from the end of the year in which that took place.

**532    Is 'made available to the public' the same as 'published'?**

Not quite. In the context of a film it means being shown in public or included in a broadcast or cable television programme.

**533    Sometimes there is nobody particular responsible for making a film. What happens about copyright then?**

If it is not possible say that anyone took on the distinctive responsibilities in paragraph 528 then none of these rules applies and copyright expires 50 years from the end of the year in which the film was made.

**534    Does the soundtrack of a film count as a sound recording or a film?**

The soundtrack of a film counts as part of the film and therefore receives the length of protection of the film, not just as a sound recording.

## Fair dealing

**535    Is there fair dealing in films?**

There is fair dealing in film or video only for the specific cases mentioned below.

**536    What about fair dealing in film or video for research for a non-commercial purpose or private study?**

There is no fair dealing in films or videos for research for a non-commercial purpose or private study.

**537 What about fair dealing in film and video for reporting current events?**
See paragraph 202 and following.

**538 And fair dealing in film or video for criticism and review?**
See paragraph 198.

## Library and archive copying

**539 Can libraries or archives copy films or videos in their collections?**
In general, no. The special provisions for library and archive copying apply only to literary, dramatic or musical works but not to other works.

**540 What is to be done for a researcher who needs a copy of part of a film or video?**
The copy cannot be supplied unless the copyright in the material is owned by the library or archive or the original copyright owner has given permission for copies to be made.

**541 Can they make copies for other archives?**
Not under copyright law, but they may have other agreements with production companies which allow this.

## Other restrictions

### Educational use

**542 Can films be copied for classroom use?**
No. But there is an exception for training in the making of films or film soundtracks and then only by the teacher or

pupil themselves and also for a non-commercial purpose. But they can be played or viewed by the class as they are broadcast.

**543 What about using films in the classroom?**
If a film or video is shown in the classroom entirely for educational purposes and only pupils and staff are present, this is not considered a public performance and is allowed.

## Copying as a condition of export

**544 Can films be copied as a condition of export?**
See paragraph 348.

## Public administration

**545 Can films be copied for public administration?**
See paragraph 350.

## Material open to public inspection

**546 Can films that are open to public inspection be copied?**
See paragraph 352.

## Multimedia

**547 If a publication contains material in several different forms such as a booklet, computer program and video, how is the copyright worked out?**
The copyright will subsist separately in each item and the rules for that format will apply. So the copyright in the entire package could run out at several different times. In that sense, it is no different from a periodical issue. It may also be a database (see Section 9).

## 548   Who is the author of a mixed-media package?

The rules for ownership and authorship are the same as for each of the components. However, the publisher will almost certainly own copyright in the format of the whole package.

# 8

# Broadcasts

Most matters relating to broadcasts, from a library and archive point of view, are dealt with under either 'sound recordings' or 'films'. However, the section on databases should also be consulted.

## Definition

### 549 What is the definition of a broadcast?

The definition of a broadcast is an electronic transmission of visual images, sounds or other information that:

- is transmitted for simultaneous reception by members of the public and is capable of lawfully being received by them, or
- is transmitted at a time determined solely by the person making the transmission for presentation to members of the public.

**550 Some people used to say websites were broadcasting. Is this still true?**

No. The law specifically states that any internet transmission is excluded from the definition of a broadcast unless it is:

- a transmission taking place simultaneously on the internet and by other means
- a concurrent transmission of a live event
- a transmission of recorded moving images or sounds forming part of a programme service offered by the person responsible for making the transmission, and is part of a service transmitted at scheduled times determined by that person.

As mentioned in Section 4, broadcasting, in a nutshell, takes precedence over internet transmission when determining the status of a transmitted work.

**551 So are cable programme services included?**

Yes, a cable programme service now fits in the definition of a broadcast although it used to be a separate class of material.

## Authorship

**552 Who is the author of a broadcast?**

Essentially it is the person who transmits the programme if that person has any responsibility for its contents.

**553 Does the author enjoy moral rights?**

Once again, in a word, no!

## Ownership of copyright

**554 Who owns the copyright in a broadcast?**

Usually the person who transmits the programme.

**555  What about a broadcast that includes a record?**

There are separate copyrights in the broadcast and the sound recording included in it. In the same way a television programme that includes a film has separate copyrights in the television transmission and the film in the programme.

**556  As broadcasts often come from many different countries, which one is regarded as the original?**

The country where the uninterrupted signal started is regarded as the country of origin.

**557  Supposing it is a satellite broadcast?**

New legislation makes it clear that where the satellite is merely a re-transmission point it has no significance in determining where the broadcast came from.

## Owners' rights

**558  What rights do owners have?**

Owners have the same rights as in literary, etc. works. See Section 3.

## Communicating the work to the public

**559  How does the right of communicating the work to the public fit in?**

By making a broadcast of any work, not only is a broadcast created, but the right of communicating the work to the public is also brought into play. So to broadcast anything requires the consent of the copyright owner. Similarly, putting anything on the internet is also an act requiring the permission of the copyright owner.

## Lending and rental

**560 How is lending and rental relevant to broadcasts?**
Although this may not seem relevant to broadcasts, copies of broadcasts that may be lent or rented must be considered as copies of those broadcasts, even though they also constitute sound recordings of films. Lending of recordings made under Educational Recording Agency (ERA) and Open University (OU) licences may be restricted. Copies made under the legislation must not be transmitted to persons outside the establishment, so this might prevent copies of broadcasts being lent to students who might then take them home or elsewhere off the premises. The law is not clear on this point.

## Publication right

**561 How does publication right apply to broadcasts?**
This is not relevant to broadcasts.

## Duration of copyright

**562 When does the copyright in a broadcast expire?**
Copyright in a broadcast expires 50 years after the year when the broadcast was made or the programme was included in a cable television service.

**563 What about repeats?**
The fact that a programme was repeated does not extend or renew the copyright.

## Fair dealing

**564 Is there fair dealing in broadcasts?**
Fair dealing in broadcasts is allowed for reporting current events and for criticism and review. The source of the broadcast

must be acknowledged where possible.

**565 Supposing I want to record something because I am out and will miss it or it clashes with another programme I want to watch or hear?**

Copying from the radio or television for personal use to listen or view at a more convenient time is allowed provided that the copy is used only for private purposes and the copying is done on your own domestic premises. This is technically called 'time-shifting'.

**566 Supposing I ask friends round to watch the recording?**

Provided they were friends or relations and you did not make any charge, this would be legal.

**567 Supposing I just want to take a photo of a TV broadcast, perhaps because it has someone I know on it?**

A single copy of an image from a broadcast for private and domestic use is allowed but it must not be copied further.

## Educational copying

**568 Can broadcasts be copied for classroom use, too?**

This must be done either with the appropriate licence or under the law as described below. Such licences are now generally available for educational establishments. See Section 10. One exception is for training in the making of films or film sound-tracks and then only by the teacher or pupil themselves. But they can be played or viewed by the class as they are broadcast.

**569 Are all broadcasts licensed?**

No. ERA licenses educational establishments to copy broadcasts from BBC, ITV and Channel 5, and the OU issues licences for its own broadcasts, but not from cable or satellite broadcasts or broadcasts from outside the UK. These broadcasts may be freely recorded as the law states that, where no licence is offered, recording is legitimate for educational use.

## 570 Are there any restrictions?

If you copy under an ERA or OU licence you must observe the limits of that licence. Other copying is subject to the following conditions:

- The source of the broadcast must be acknowledged.
- The educational purpose must be non-commercial.
- The copy of the broadcast must not be transmitted to any person outside the premises of the establishment.

## 571 Can recordings of these broadcasts be lent to students?

This is debatable. Such broadcasts must not be transmitted to people off the premises, which would include distance learning students and many working in virtual learning environments (VLEs). So lending a copy to a student might mean it is taken off the premises, which would have the same effect. But the term 'transmitted' is not defined.

## 572 Does this mean that organizations that are not considered educational can make off-air recordings?

Yes, provided the purpose of the education is non-commercial.

## 573 What does 'non-commercial' mean?

It is not defined but would exclude any course organized by a commercial or industrial company for its employees, and any course where the fees were fixed at a level that would generate some kind of profit rather than cost-recovery.

## Library and archive copying

## 574 Can libraries and archives record off-air for their collections?

This is permitted only for specified collections which at the time of writing are: the British Film Institute, the British Library, the British Medical Association, the British Music Information Centre, the Imperial War Museum, the Music Performance Research Centre, the National Library of Wales and the Scottish Film Council.

**575  Can other archives keep off-air recordings made for 'time-shifting' purposes?**
No. They must be kept and used by the person who made them for their own use. Only designated archives can retain material for archival purposes. Copies made under ERA licences are a different matter and can be kept indefinitely. OU broadcasts usually have conditions relating to the time they are kept and notification of this to the OU attached to them.

**576  Supposing someone's papers are deposited with an archive and these papers include copies of audiovisual materials such as off-air recordings? Can the archive keep these?**
In theory, no. They are infringing copies because off-air recording can be done only for certain limited purposes and storing the copies in an archive is not one of them.

# Databases

## Definitions

**577 What is the definition of a database?**

A database is defined as: 'a collection of works, data or other materials which are arranged in a systematic or methodical way and are individually accessible by electronic or other means'.

**578 Are databases protected by copyright?**

Databases can certainly be subject to copyright but they are now also subject to a quite separate database right.

**579 Can a literary work also be a database?**

Yes, it can. In order to be recognized as a literary work, a database will be eligible only if it is original (a vital test for copyright protection) and the selection of the contents and arrangement of the database constitutes the author's own intellectual creation. In this case the database will acquire both copyright and database right protection.

**580    Must a database be electronic to be protected?**
Definitely not. The phrase 'other means' makes it quite clear.

## Copyright and database right

A database can be subject to both copyright and database right and it is very important to remember this when reading the following paragraphs.

**581    What is the difference between copyright and database right?**
Essentially, a database is subject to copyright if it is a work of personal intellectual activity; otherwise it does not attract copyright but does attract the new database right. If someone devotes their entire academic life to compiling an annotated bibliography on a particular subject with comments, evaluations and selection of materials, then this would attract copyright. A monthly bibliography on the same subject produced by library staff without any real selective judgement and with no one author would merely be a database.

**582    Are all databases now protected by database right?**
Basically, yes.

**583    How does something qualify for database right?**
To qualify for database right the contents of the database must have been assembled as the result of substantial investment in obtaining, verifying or presenting the contents.

**584    Does investment just mean money?**
No. Investment specifically includes financial, human or technical resources.

**585    If the database is made up of material that is not copyright, is the database still protected?**

Yes, if it qualifies as a database. The copyright status of the content of a database is irrelevant. It is the construction of the database that is the key question. The following table might help to clarify this rather complex situation.

| Content | Arrangement | Select, verify, present | Protection ©=copyright; DR = database right; X = no protection | Example |
|---------|-------------|-------------------------|------------------------------------------------------------------|---------|
| Copyright | Original | Yes | © © DR | *Chemical Abstracts* |
| Copyright | Not original | Yes | © X DR | *Books in Print* |
| Copyright | Original | No* | © © X | Existing collection of recent papers rearranged by subject |
| Copyright | Not original | No | © X X | Collection of author's own papers by date |
| Not copyright | Original | Yes | X © DR | Selected 18th century sermons by subject |
| Not copyright | Not original | Yes | X X DR | Telephone white pages |
| Not copyright | Original | No* | X © X | Existing collection of 18th century papers rearranged by subject |
| Not copyright | Not original | No | X X X | Tough! |

*It seems unlikely that this situation could happen as arrangement or rearrangement would probably result in a different form of presentation.

## Authorship

**586   Who is the author of a database?**

Apart from the fairly rare occasion when a database has a personal author (see paragraph 66), the author is defined as the maker of the database. The maker of a database is the person who takes the initiative in obtaining, verifying or presenting the contents of the database and assumes the risk of investing in those actions and therefore obtains the database right. Makers cannot qualify for this right unless they are individuals with EEA nationality, companies or organizations incorporated within the EEA, or partnerships or unincorporated bodies formed under the law of an EEA state.

## Moral rights

**587   Are there moral rights in databases?**

There are no moral rights in databases unless they are the creation of an individual person when the usual rules about derogatory treatment would apply.

## Ownership of copyright and database right

**588   Who owns copyright and database right?**

Where copyright subsists, the copyright rules apply (see Section 3). Ownership of database right belongs to the maker of the database, although the usual rules about ownership of works made as part of employment or for the Crown apply.

## Duration of copyright and database right

**589   How long do the rights in databases last?**

When a database attracts copyright protection the usual rules of duration of copyright for literary works apply (see paragraph 144 and following). When database right applies, this lasts for

15 years from the end of the year in which the database was completed. If, during that time, it is made available to the public, then the 15-year term runs from the end of the year in which the database was made available.

**590 But databases are constantly being updated. What happens to the length of protection then?**

If substantial changes, including accumulation of data, additions or deletions, take place so that the new database would be considered the subject of substantial new investment, then the 15-year period will begin again. In other words, where a database is frequently being updated it will remain protected by database right for 15 years after the final changes have been made.

**591 What about old databases?**

Where a database was completed after 1 January 1983 and the database right began to operate when the regulations came into force, then that database obtains database right until 31 December 2013.

**592 What about databases that already exist but which would not qualify for copyright under the new rules?**

If the database was made before 27 March 1996 and was copyright immediately before the regulations came into force, then it remains in copyright under the usual rules for copyright duration.

## Owners' rights

**593 What rights does the owner of copyright and database right enjoy?**

The rights that owners have in the copyright of a database are much the same as those for literary, dramatic and musical works (see paragraph 48 and following). The rights of database rights owners are defined in a different way.

### 594   What rights does the owner of database right have?

The owner of the database right has the right to prevent the extraction or reuse of all or a substantial part of the contents of the database.

### 595   What precisely does 'extraction' mean?

The word 'extraction' is defined as 'permanent or temporary transfer of the contents to another medium by any means or in any form'.

### 596   Does this mean that nothing can ever be taken from a database?

No. A user is allowed to extract small amounts of data provided that the amount taken is insubstantial.

### 597   What counts as insubstantial?

This is not defined but in deciding if the amount taken is substantial or not, quality and quantity are both factors, separately and together. So it is possible to take a small quantity but still infringe the database right because of the quality of what has been taken. The reverse is also true.

*Example*: It might be considered that three or four entries from different parts of the 'white' telephone pages is not substantial but to take the addresses of all four companies listed in the *Yellow Pages* under a highly specific classification could be substantial.

### 598   Supposing someone copies an insubstantial amount one day and then does the same a few days later? Is this allowed?

No. The law has spotted this cunning ploy. It specifies that systematic extraction of insubstantial parts of a database may amount to extraction of substantial amounts. In other words, extractions done at different times must be seen as cumulative.

**599 What about 're-utilization'? Does this stop me using any information?**

No. 'Re-utilization' is defined as 'making the contents available to the public by any means'. Re-utilization (or reuse) is dealt with under 'fair dealing' (see paragraph 603 and following).

**600 Surely this is making facts subject to copyright?**

Not really. Copyright and the other rights associated with it refer to using someone else's property. Imagine someone has compiled a list of ice-cream makers in east coast resorts. There is nothing to stop someone else compiling their own list and issuing this as a free or commercial product provided they have compiled it from scratch and not used the other person's list. The idea behind database right is to give some protection to the person who invested in putting the data together in the first place, not to give them exclusive control over those facts but the way those facts have been assembled and made available.

**601 What about other rights such as copying, issuing to the public and so on?**

These are really covered by the right to prevent extraction and reuse. Other rights such as performance, publication right or making available right (see paragraph 687) would not apply to databases.

## Fair dealing

**602 Are databases subject to fair dealing in the same way as literary works?**

Yes, but with an important difference. Where a database is *copyright* then it is subject to fair dealing for research for a non-commercial purpose or private study provided the source is indicated. Where the database is subject only to database right then the following rules apply.

**603   Does this mean that if I find some information I can at least use it?**

Yes, on two counts. First, if you need to use a substantial part of the database, you can do this provided that it is for non-commercial research or private study. So you can certainly look up the addresses of the five or six ice-cream manufacturers in Bridlington and Scarborough and write them down for your own use but this information cannot be issued to the public in the form of a trade directory, database or in any other way. Whether you need to write down on your piece of paper by the telephone the source of the information to comply with this rule seems highly unlikely! Secondly, if the amount taken is insubstantial and you are a lawful user of the database, you can extract *and* re-utilize this information in other words, but use it and re-package it for publication or further use. But remember that insubstantial amounts will be very small amounts indeed!

**604   Why is commercial research excluded?**

The law is quite specific that *anything* done to a database for the purposes of research for a commercial purpose is not fair dealing with that database.

**605   Is there a definition of 'commercial'?**

No. See Appendix 3 for some possible commercial or non-commercial uses.

**606   What constitutes a lawful user?**

A lawful user is someone who has a right to use the database. In a paper context this is anyone entitled to use the library where it is stored, or any private owner of a database, or anyone they permit to have access to it. In the electronic context it will be anyone who legitimately has a licence to use or be allowed to use the database.

**607 Are users of library services lawful users?**
This will depend on the licence the library has with the database owner. In electronic situations it is important to ensure the library's licence includes as wide a range of uses as possible so that nobody is excluded. For commercial companies lawful uses may be a much more restricted group (such as company employees only or even only those in the R&D department).

**608 Some electronic databases come with very strict licences. Can these prevent any use of the database at all?**
Not legally. The terms of any contract that aims to prevent a lawful user from extracting or reusing insubstantial parts of the database will be considered null and void in law.

## Educational copying

**609 Can databases be copied for educational purposes?**
Where a database is protected only by copyright then the usual rules apply. Where database right exists this is not infringed if a substantial part is extracted for the purposes of illustration for teaching or research and this is not done for any commercial purpose and the source is acknowledged.

**610 Does this mean to illustrate research?**
This is not at all clear. Whether 'illustration' belongs with teaching or 'teaching and research' is not stated. The words given are those from the law – only a judge may ever sort this out!

## Library and archive copying

**611 Can databases be made available through libraries?**
Essentially the answer is 'yes'. Certainly under a licence from the database owner this can be done but it is essential to ensure that all legitimate users of the library are designated as 'lawful users', otherwise they do not have the right to use any of the

material in the database. If the database is in paper format, problems of access do not arise in copyright terms but the issue of what users may copy will remain.

**612    Can libraries copy parts of databases for users?**
Where a database is copyright (only) then libraries may copy it as they can other library works (a reasonable proportion); however, library copying is not permitted for database right so the abilities of libraries to copy in this respect are limited to copying an insubstantial part.

# Other restrictions

## Adaptation

**613    Supposing someone took a database, altered the way it was arranged and then re-issued it? Would that be allowed?**
This is not allowed, as the law specifically defines adaptation as including arrangement or alteration of the version or translation.

## Lending and rental

**614    Presumably libraries cannot lend databases?**
Yes, they can. It is easy to think that database = electronic database, but these rules apply to paper copies too. So, the lending of a database as defined by paragraph 577 is not considered as extraction or reuse and is therefore allowed under the same conditions as literary works. Similarly on-the-spot reference is permitted. See paragraphs 112–13 for lending and rental.

## Making copies available for public inspection

**615    Can databases be made available for public inspection?**
Similar rules to those for literary works apply to databases.

## Public administration

**616 Can databases be made available for the purpose of public administration?**
Similar rules to those for literary works apply to databases.

## Visually impaired people

**617 Can databases be made available in alternative formats for VIPs?**
Not under the current law because this was introduced as a result of EU legislation, which specifically excluded any changes to existing laws relating to databases. However, the industry guidelines on making materials available for VIPs is much more generous and does not exclude databases. Consult www.pls.org.uk for more details on industry guidelines in this area.

# Licensing schemes

The situation relating to licensing schemes is changing all the time. What is given in this section is simply an outline of the major schemes, how they work and what benefits and limitations they bring. Details of individual licensing schemes need to be obtained from the relevant agency or organization. Details of appropriate websites and addresses are given in Appendix 1. The outline information in this chapter is current in Spring 2004.

## 618   What is a licensing scheme?

Basically it is a scheme that allows someone, who is not the copyright owner, to use copyright material beyond the limits of the law with the permission of the copyright owner. They are administered by different organizations and these can change. They are briefly described in the following paragraphs.

## 619   What is the difference between a licensing scheme and a licence?

A licensing scheme is one that covers a defined range of works and is offered to a particular class of organization (government departments, academic institutions), and that anyone who is in the class named can join. So a scheme for universities must be open to any university to join it. A licence is more often an agreement between the copyright owner, often represented by a copyright agency, and an individual user. Their terms may be similar to a licensing scheme but are usually tailored to the specific needs of the user.

**620 Are licensing schemes relevant to libraries?**

Certainly, because any licence held by the organization that owns or administers the library will almost certainly include copying done in the library. But it is unusual for licensing schemes to be only for the library. The library is part of a larger organization, which is licensed as a whole. The library must abide by the terms of any licences as they represent a contract between the licensing agency and the licensee.

**621 What are the details of such schemes?**

Each scheme will vary according to the type of material covered and the type of organization holding the licence. The terms and conditions of licences vary from one type of organization to another and from time to time so anything said here about the terms of a licence should be checked with the licensing agency before a licence is considered. These notes are for general guidance only. Note too that a licence is a contract and the terms of the contract are what count in the end, not advice or comments in a general book on copyright such as this one!

**622 Many journals have details of payment to the Copyright Clearance Center in the USA printed on the bottom of the page. Must libraries pay these fees to CCC?**

Payment should be made only if copying is done beyond what UK law permits. The Copyright Licensing Agency

(CLA) currently acts as the agent for the CCC and they should be contacted in cases of doubt. The national copyright agencies work together to form an international network through which payments are transferred.

### 623    What about copying publications from other countries?
The CLA has agreements with a number of countries to collect royalties on behalf of copyright owners in those countries. An up-to-date list can be obtained from the CLA.

### 624    What are the major licensing agencies and schemes?
The brief description below gives a general idea of each agency and the type of licence it offers. Specific details should be obtained from the appropriate agency.

### 625    Copyright Licensing Agency
The Copyright Licensing Agency is the largest agency that libraries will encounter. It offers a range of licences to copy onto and from paper and can now offer licences for fax copying as well, which is technically electronic copying. Some licences currently offer making scanned copies and putting them onto a secure intranet site. Again, see the CLA website for details. The CLA also has an agreement with the Design and Artists Copyright Society (DACS) so the CLA can now offer a licence that includes artistic works. These are some examples:

> *Educational copying*: The licence allows one copy of one article from a periodical issue or 5% of a book or one chapter; one copy for each pupil in a class and one for the teacher, whether school, college or university. Libraries may also be allowed to make one copy of such material for the short-loan collection. Separate licences currently exist for local education authority schools, independent schools, further education colleges and higher education institutions (HEIs). As details vary, consult the CLA website for details.

*Government departments*: Licences are structured according to the needs of the department.

*Industry and commerce*: A model licence was negotiated with the Confederation of British Industry (CBI), which they could recommend to their members (but could not negotiate it for them). This is essentially a matrix consisting of the sector in which the company operates and the number of research staff they employ. A similar licence has been negotiated for legal firms with the Law Society. There is also a special licence for regulatory material required by the pharmaceutical industry. These licences often include scanning UK publications and putting the image onto a secure intranet site.

Other licences have been issued for the NHS, local authorities and learned societies. It is likely that licences will be available to all sectors in the near future.

## 626 Does the licence cover copying for visually-impaired people?
The CLA licence includes the making of copies in large print, Braille and Moon but not audio.

## 627 What about providing copies to people outside my organization?
The CLA currently (spring 2004) offers three document delivery licences:

- Transactional Document Delivery Licence
- Low Volume Document Delivery Licence
- Sticker scheme.

## 628 What are the differences?
The *Transactional Document Delivery Licence* allows any library to provide copies of documents for commercial research. It is

designed for libraries that delivery more than 100 copies a month. Copyright fees are set individually by publishers. The *Low Volume Document Delivery Licence* is intended for libraries that deliver fewer than 100 copies a month for commercial purposes. There is a flat copyright fee. The *sticker scheme* is intended for libraries that have walk-in users who are not employees or members of the institution. For example, anyone using a public library or a member of the general public using a university library. This scheme is also a flat fee one. The library collects the fee from the user and passes it to the CLA with bibliographic details of the works covered.

### 629   Why cannot an employee of a company with a CLA licence simply go into a public library and make a copy under the firm's licence?

The CLA licence only covers material, copies of which are owned by the organization holding the licence. So anything in the public library of which the company did not own its own copy would not be covered.

### 630   Christian Copyright Licensing International

The CCLI offers a licence for the copying of both the words and music of many hymns. Licences are available for churches, schools and conference centres but the original work must be owned by the licensor. Borrowing copies from a library outside the licensed organization and then copying is not covered by the licence. The scheme is remarkable as the first to license copying of music of any kind.

### 631   The Newspaper Licensing Agency

The NLA offers a range of licences to different sectors. There is a standard copying licence but separate terms. Currently the licence covers:

• all UK national newspapers

- over 800 of the biggest regional papers such as *Yorkshire Post*, *Manchester Evening News* and *Scotsman*
- the Lloyd's List
- titles from France, the Republic of Ireland, the Netherlands, Norway, Switzerland and the US.

## 632  What does the NLA licence allow?

The NLA licence allows:

- photocopying, faxing and digitally reproducing press cuttings
- use for internal management purposes
- copying for educational purposes
- in certain cases copying to members and clients.

## 633  Can someone with an NLA licence copy material in other libraries?

Yes. Unlike the CLA licence the NLA licence covers the copying of all the newspapers licensed, regardless of whether the licensee owns a copy of them or not.

## 634  The Design and Artists Copyright Society

This licence is slightly different from others in that it legitimizes existing infringing collections of slides in educational establishments as well as licensing the making of new slides. Organizations joining the Society declare their infringing collections and pay a one-off fee for these; there is then an annual licence fee based on the number of slides made. The scheme includes all artistic works as listed on the DACS website, including those published in books, and DACS offers an indemnity in the case of users being challenged. DACS also has an arrangement for licensing artistic works through the CLA licensing system.

## 635  The Educational Recording Agency

The ERA offers a licence for educational establishments only for off-air recording of all terrestrial broadcasting. As there is no licence for cable or satellite broadcasting at present, these programmes may be freely recorded for educational purposes only. Once recorded, a copy may be used for teaching and further copied within the terms of the licence. It may be kept in the library of the institution for which it was recorded. Licensed items must be labelled as such and may be lent only in exceptional circumstances within the terms of the ERA licence. Recording does not have to be done on the premises – it could be done by a teacher or lecturer at home for subsequent use within the licensed premises.

## 636   The Open University Educational Enterprises

The OUEE licence is clearly specific for OU output. Again it is available only to educational establishments. Payment is according to the number of recordings kept for more than 30 days. Recordings kept for fewer than 30 days are not paid for, but all recordings must be registered.

## 637   HMSO

Recent changes in government policy mean that many documents published, or controlled, by HMSO may now be freely copied. Most legislation and similar material, many official reports and documents can all be copied and reused. Single and multiple copies are allowed and documents may be included in other works (such as textbooks) and they can be included in websites and other publications. The Royal Coat of Arms may not be included as this has become a sort of trademark or guarantee of integrity. As this is a rapidly changing area, it is best to consult the HMSO website for the latest guidance. See the website (www.hmso.gov.uk/guides.htm).

## 638   Ordnance Survey

Because maps are artistic works, copying of these by libraries is not permitted although individuals may claim fair dealing. The

OS has introduced a wide range of licences for education, local authorities, commercial and business, legal procedures and planning permissions. They are very detailed and liable to quite radical change from time to time and it would be misleading to describe them all here. The most important one for the general public and public libraries is that OS allows a library to supply copies or a member of the public to make copies up to the following limits: four copies may be made provided they are from a single map and that no more than 625 cm² (A4 size) are made and this is at the original size – no enlargements are allowed. There are separate schemes for local authority and planning applications and libraries are advised not to get involved in copying for these purposes as they may not be aware of the finer points of the agreement. Details of educational, commercial and other types of licence should be obtained from OS direct.

## 639  British Standards Institution

BSI issue special licences for classroom use. In the case of Standards in public collections BSI has stated that it regards up to 10% of a standard can be copied without infringement.

## 640  British Library Document Supply Centre

The British Library Document Supply Centre (BLDSC) holds a licence from the CLA which allows it to make copies similar to the transactional licence described above (see paragraph 628). Basically, when a copy is supplied through this service the following limitations normally imposed on library copying do not apply so that:

- more than one copy of an item can be supplied
- more than one article from an issue of a periodical can be supplied
- signed declarations are not required
- non-prescribed libraries can behave as if they are prescribed

libraries (adding material to stock, obtaining replacement material, and so on)
- fees to end-users need not be charged
- the purpose does not necessarily have to be for research or private study
- copies may be for research for a non-commercial purpose.

Copies may not be further copied except under the strict terms of any CLA licence held by the organization receiving the copies.

## 641   British Phonographic Industries

Public libraries may not lend sound recordings except under licence and such a licence was negotiated by The Library Association with the BPI for public libraries (only). This is based on a combination of the number of copies of any one work held at any one service point and a 'holdback' period for new releases when they will not be lent. The agreement covers vinyl, CD and cassettes but not other forms of digital recording. There is no licence fee. Currently (spring 2004) the Spoken Word Publishers Association (SWPA) is stepping outside this agreement and seeking a separate agreement in the light of the new legislation on lending and rental. Similarly, representatives of performers are also seeking compensation through a licensing scheme. Contact CILIP for the latest position.

## 642   The Performing Right Society

The PRS is one of the oldest licensing societies in the world. It licenses all public performances of music whether these are live or recorded, including public use of radios and television.

## 643   The Mechanical Copyright Protection Society

The MCPS licenses the recording of music onto any medium and re-recording of music from abroad. Essentially MCPS licenses the making of a recording, PRS licenses the public performance of that music, and PPL licenses the public use of the recording.

### 644    Phonographic Performance Ltd

PPL is a music industry collecting society representing over 2500 record companies, from the large multinationals to the small independents. They collect licence fees from broadcast and *public* performance users on behalf of the record companies. This licence fee revenue, after deduction of running costs, is then distributed to record company members and to performers.

## Other licences

There is an increasingly bewildering array of licences and permissions systems available. They include the Joint Information Systems Committee/Publishers Association guidelines and UK-wide Higher Education Funding Council for England licence; the National Electronic Site Licence (NESLI) and Higher Education on Demand (HERON). Also, many individual publishers have their own tailor-made licences for different situations. It is impossible to do more than indicate that these exist and users should follow them up as necessary.

# 11

# Computer programs, electronic materials and websites

It is very important to distinguish between electronic material and databases. One is the format in which a work is stored or transmitted, the other is a form of a work itself. There are many works that are electronic but not databases and equally many databases that are not electronic! This chapter tries to deal with some of these questions but users of this book should realize that this is a constantly changing situation and the subject matter, questions and answers are all moving targets. Because the term 'electronic materials' can cover works in electronic form, computer programs and databases, these items will be dealt with separately within the usual headings in this chapter although they are all linked together in some respects.

**645** There are many copyright questions that arise in the electronic world to which the answers are exactly the same as in the more traditional paper-based world. However, some issues are peculiar to electronic materials and some of the answers that are quite clear in the paper world are not so obvious when we deal with electronic materials. The introduction of new legislation on databases makes many of the answers different if the work is considered a database.

## Computer programs

**646 Are computer programs a separate sort of work?**
In some ways but not in others. Although computer programs are classed as literary works, there are some special conditions that apply.

**647 What about computer programs that have been printed out?**
These are literary works. (See Section 4.) As a lot of work goes into preparing the design of a computer program, this is protected as well. It would in any case be considered as a literary work, but the law does specify this type of work as being protected.

**648 Who is the author of a computer program?**
The person who wrote the program.

**649 How long does copyright in a computer program last?**
The same as a literary work (see Section 4).

**650 What rights does the copyright owner of a computer program have?**
Basically, the same as in a literary work (see Section 4).

**651 Are there any special rules?**
It is worth noting that translation of a computer program in-

cludes transferring it from one computer language to another. But see the following paragraph.

### 652   Are computer programs subject to fair dealing?

Yes, but just how this could work in practice is difficult to determine. One area where a sort of fair dealing exists is to allow the translation of a lower language program into a higher language. Strangely, the law excludes this activity under fair dealing but specifically allows it in another part of the legislation! This must be done by a lawful user of the program.

### 653   What about making back-up copies?

If a lawful user needs to make a back-up copy for lawful use of the program then this is not an infringement of copyright. 'Lawful use' is not defined.

### 654   Supposing a programmer wants to use the program to create a quite separate program? Can the program be decompiled for this purpose?

Yes, provided that the necessary conditions are met. These are that the information obtained through decompiling the program is not used for any other purpose than creating an independent program, which must not be similar to the one decompiled. In addition, the information must not be passed on to anyone unless they need to know for the purposes of creating the new program, nor must the information be readily available through any other source.

### 655   Sometimes contracts forbid some of the copying outlined in the previous paragraphs. Can anything be done?

Yes, the law specifically states that where a contract tries to prevent any of these actions then that element of the contract is null and void.

## Educational copying

### 656 Can computer programs be copied for educational purposes?

Only with the consent of the copyright owner directly or under licence. Some software is made available specifically for educational purposes and is free of copyright restrictions provided it is not exploited for commercial purposes. The exceptions for setting examination questions would seem to apply to computer programs as to other copyright works.

## Library and archive copying

### 657 Can computer programs be copied by libraries and archives for their users?

No, unless it is possible to determine what is a reasonable proportion of a computer program and it could then be copied for the reader as part of a non-periodical work (see paragraph 254). In practice the answer is simply 'no'.

### 658 What happens if the library has a computer program or other electronic material which becomes unusable for technical reasons? Can it be copied so that it can continue to be used?

Yes, provided that the conditions of purchase do not prohibit such copying and the original copy must not be retained, otherwise it becomes an infringing copy.

## Broadcasting

### 659 How does broadcasting apply to computer programs?

This is not really applicable to computer programs. Where a work is in electronic format the same rules apply as if it were in paper format.

## Lending and rental

**660   Can computer programs be lent or rented out?**
They can be lent, other than by public libraries, but cannot be
rented without the copyright owner's consent. See paragraph 113.

# Electronic materials

**661   Are electronic materials defined in legal terms?**
Yes. 'Electronic' means actuated by electric, magnetic, electromag-
netic, electro-chemical or electromechanical energy, and 'in electronic form' means in a form usable only by electronic means.

**662   So are electronic materials a separate group of protected
works?**
No. What is protected is the content of the electronic material and
the electronic version of it. This is just like a paper copy where the
contents of a book are protected but so is the typography.

**663   But electronic materials always need some software to
make them work. Is this part of the copyright in the
work?**
No. It is important to distinguish between the content of the
work and the supporting computer systems. The latter will be
copyright in their own right as computer software. It would be
possible, for example, to have an electronic document that was
out of copyright but software which was certainly still protected.

## Computer-generated works

**664   Some works are generated automatically by computer, so
who is the author of a computer-generated work?**
The law says it is the person by whom the arrangements necessary for the creation of the work were undertaken.

**665   Is it really possible for a work to be totally computer-generated?**

This is open to debate. Although there are documents that can be generated automatically, somewhere along the line a human person set up the program to generate the work or at least gave the computer some instructions on how this should be done subsequently.

**666   How long does the copyright in a computer-generated work last?**

The copyright in a computer-generated work expires 70* years from the end of the year in which the work was made.

## Authorship of electronic materials

**667   Who is the author of an electronic work?**

The author of the content of an electronic work will be decided in the same way as if that work were not electronic. In other words: if it is an electronic text, think of it as a book or periodical article; if it is a picture, consider whether it is a photograph or painting, and so on.

## Moral rights

**668   Do authors of electronic materials enjoy moral rights?**

Yes, in exactly the same way as in other materials. But since it is unlikely that a book or film will be released only in electronic form the moral right to be named as the author in these two cases is equally unlikely to arise. However, the internet may be used to create artistic works where authors do have the right to have their name attached to a work when exhibited in public.

**669   If the work is scanned or digitized who will be the author of the electronic version?**

It is unlikely that the scanned or digitized version of a work will have an individual author. Unless one can specifically be identified, the electronic version will be considered anonymous and the rules for anonymous works will apply.

### 670   Does authorship really matter in electronic documents?

Yes, and it will become a vital issue. Researchers and users generally want to know who was responsible for a document, database or any other work as this has a bearing on its importance and value; it also gives an idea of the point of view behind an author's work. It is possible now to use technology to link authorship to payment. Anyway, those who write really do want the credit, even if there is no money involved.

### 671   Do authors of electronic materials enjoy moral rights?

Yes, and they are very important in an electronic context. It is easy to change content or authorship, or conceal the origin of a work in an electronic context and all of these are moral rights enjoyed by authors. Essentially the same rules apply as for the paper world.

## Ownership

### 672   What are the rules for ownership of electronic works?

The rules for ownership of electronic works are the same as for materials in printed format.

### 673   Do owners enjoy the same rights for electronic materials as they do for paper materials?

Broadly, yes but with some very important additions and one or two changes.

### 674   What about copying?

This is an exclusive right of the owner.

**675   But surely every use of an electronic document involves copying? Does this mean that all such copying is an infringement?**

Fortunately not. The original 1988 Act gave the owner the exclusive right to control the making of transient or incidental copies even if these were essential to some legitimate use of the work. Therefore to call something up on a website would technically be an infringement as you cause the work to be copied to the internet service provider (ISP) and then to your own hard disk. The new legislation prevents the copyright owner from enforcing copyright in such temporary copies provided that:

- They are a necessary part of the technical process to transfer the information.
- The transfer is between third parties (website→ISP→end-user).
- The temporary copy does not have any independent economic significance.

**676   What would constitute a copy with economic significance?**

The law does not say but if you send someone a fax and the person receiving it prints it out immediately then the intermediate digital copies are not significant. But if you stored the message so it could be re-transmitted to lots of other people in your organization, that would certainly have an independent economic significance.

**677   Who has the right to issue copies to the public?**

This is an exclusive right of the copyright owner and needs to be interpreted in the context of online activity and physical carriers such as CD-ROMs or DVDs.

**678   Who has the right to perform, show or play the work?**

These rights are the same as for literary, dramatic and musical works.

**679 Who has the right to adapt or translate the work?**

These rights are the same as for literary, dramatic and musical works.

## Lending and rental

**680 Can electronic materials be rented?**

Rental, as for all other copyright works, is an exclusive right of the copyright owner and this includes both works in electronic form and computer programs as such.

**681 What about lending electronic materials?**

From a legal point of view, computer programs and works in electronic form can be lent. In practice, these products are usually sold with restrictions included in the contract so that they cannot be lent or used on premises other than those specified in the contract. If there is no specific contract then it should be possible to lend, for example, a CD-ROM within the limits for lending specified in paragraphs 112 and 113.

**682 Supposing a library has a work in electronic form and another library wants to consult it? Can the second library be given access for a limited time?**

Probably not. The contract giving access will define who can use a particular electronic work.

**683 Is it meaningful to talk about lending in an electronic sense?**

Yes, for two reasons. First, electronic materials may still be on physical carriers, such as disks, and these could be physically lent. Secondly, lending really results in passing something to someone else so that the owner of it does not have use of it for a limited time while the other person does. This can now be achieved electronically by transmitting something to someone and:

- putting a 'block' on access to it while it is being used elsewhere, and
- constructing automatic erasing mechanisms so that the 'borrowing' library or person loses the work after the specified time.

Watch out for developments in this area.

## Publication right

**684 Are electronic materials generally subject to publication right?**
Theoretically, yes but where do you find such materials out of copyright!!?

## Communicate to the public right

**685 What does 'communicate to the public right' mean?**
This is a new right introduced in October 2003. In a nutshell, it allows the copyright owner to control putting the work onto a website and therefore plugs the hole in the law, which excludes transmission of a website from the definition of a broadcast.

**686 What is the actual definition of this new right?**
Making the work available by electronic transmission so that members of the public may access it from a place and at a time individually chosen by them.

## Performance

**687 Are the rights of performance relevant to electronic materials?**
Yes, in two respects. First, the content of an electronic document may be multimedia in nature with songs, speeches or dancing. These all have rights of performance in them. Secondly, perform-

ers now enjoy a separate right to prevent thief performances being made available on the internet without their permission This is called 'making available right'.

### 688   What exactly is this right, then?

It is defined as: 'Right to prevent anyone making available to the public a recording of a performance by electronic transmission so that members of the public may access the recording from a place and at a time chosen by them'.

## Duration

### 689   How long does copyright in an electronic work last?

So far as the content is concerned, the same rules apply as if the work were not electronic.

### 690   But if a new edition of a work causes a new term of copyright, what constitutes a new edition of an electronically stored work?

That is difficult to decide. Obviously if a whole new piece is added, then the work is a new edition, but if, as in the case of a database, material is added frequently, and in small pieces, it is difficult to say whether every addition creates a new edition or whether a lot of new data has to be added before this can be claimed. A further problem is that no actual printed version will be made every time a change is made, so some editions may come and go and never be known about. Special rules apply to databases.

## Copying

### *Fair dealing*

### 691   Is there fair dealing in electronic works?

This is not an easy question to answer. Technically there is fair dealing in the content of any electronic work where that content qualifies for fair dealing as a literary, dramatic, musical or artistic work. However, as electronic works can be accessed usually only by the use of passwords and a contract with the supplier, what can and cannot be done by a user is governed by the terms of that contract and the issue of the password, rather than by copyright law as such. A further consideration is what is 'fair' in electronic terms. Fair dealing is not limited to copying but this is the most usual form that it takes. But the idea of 'fair' (see paragraph 175) may be difficult to justify in an electronic world when it is so easy to reproduce a work *exactly*, store and retransmit it and even change it. Whether fair dealing generally exists in an electronic world has never been tested. It should but it may or may not, depending on the circumstances. The World Intellectual Property Organization (WIPO) – the body responsible for administering international copyright treaties – has supported the idea that fair dealing should exist in the electronic environment.

## Other purposes and limitations

### 692 Does the law permit the use of electronic materials for other purposes?

The law permits use of electronic materials for criticism or review and reporting current events in just the same way as other materials.

### 693 Are there any other limitations?

The rules for use of copyright materials for public administration and visually impaired people are the same.

## Protection mechanisms

### 694 But some electronic documents can be accessed only by using a password or giving your credit card number. Is this legal?

Yes, the law specifically protects the use of effective technological measures to protect electronic materials.

**695   What does 'effective technological measures' actually mean?**

If use of the work is controlled by the copyright owner through:

- an access control or protection process such as encryption, scrambling or other transformation of the work, or
- a copy control mechanism that achieves the intended protection,

then the protection mechanism is considered an effective one.

**696   What difference does this make?**

A lot, because it is an offence (and this can be criminal) to circumvent such effective protection mechanisms, and the copyright owner has the same redress as if the copyright of the work itself were infringed.

**697   But couldn't this stop someone from exercising the privileges they have under fair dealing or use by a visually impaired person?**

Yes, this is true.

**698   What can be done in these circumstances?**

The law provides a very cumbersome and unsatisfactory remedy in these circumstances. In summary it says that if an effective technological measure prevents a user from benefiting from exceptions such as fair dealing, library privilege, needs as a VIP or educational copying, the user shall make a complaint to the Secretary of State. The Secretary of State may give to the copyright owner or licensee such directions as seem fit to establish whether any voluntary measure of agreement already subsists that enables the complainant to benefit from the exceptions.

# Websites

**699  How do website fit in?**

Websites present all kinds of copyright problems The paragraphs below give some indication of the difficulties libraries may face when considering using website technology to develop their services. You will need to consider who owns the website and whether the website constitutes a database as defined in law. Other issues include the status of a website (whether a broadcast or a cable programme service) and liability of website providers.

**700  Is it an infringement to put works on the internet or world wide web?**

Yes. This is infringing the right of communication to the public by electronic means.

**701  But supposing a document is put on the world wide web and nobody ever downloads it? Is this still an infringement?**

Yes, because the document has been made available to the public by electronic means. The fact that nobody accesses the work is another matter. It is an infringement of communication to the public right, even if this is done without charge, unless the person issuing the copies has the right to do so. The fact that nobody ever reads these copies is irrelevant!

**702  Does the fact that it is so easy to build links to other websites pose any problems?**

Yes. If you build a link to another website it is best to obtain the permission of the website owner and to make sure the link is to the homepage and not into the body of the website text. But it also depends on whether you:

• build your link to the homepage of the other website
• build deep links (direct into the text of the other website)

- use framed links (icons to click on round the edge of the screen which obscure who actually owns the website)
- build embedded links (where an actual image from another website is embedded in your own to make the link direct).

### 703   Why go to so much trouble?
Because:

- The website owner may not wish their website to be associated with yours – you may be promoting views with which they strongly disagree.
- You may bypass important information about ownership, conditions of use and even advertising, all of which the user would have found on the homepage.
- If the user does not perceive that the information is owned by and made available through a different website provider from the one where the reader began the search, the reader may think the material is owned or supplied by the original website to which they logged on. This can cause the library to be accused of 'passing-off' – making services available that users think come from the library when, in fact, they belong to someone else.

### 704   Some websites have an icon to click for copyright information. Is this legal or necessary?
It is very necessary to ensure that users know exactly who owns what and what the user can do with material located. The icon prevents the user from claiming ignorance of either ownership or conditions. Where websites start with a statement such as 'By clicking on this icon you agree that you have read the conditions of use and copyright statement' then the user is bound by those conditions and cannot plead ignorance.

### 705   Is all material on the web copyright?
Probably. To be safe, behave with material on the web as if it were

in paper form. If you would not copy or distribute it in paper form, then do not do it in electronic form. That is, unless the owner specifically states this can be done – which many website owners do.

## 706 What about older text such as medieval manuscripts, which have been put on the web by major libraries or archives?

The original text may be out of copyright but the electronic version will almost certainly attract its own copyright as it will have been created as a result of extensive research, editing and correction. Electronic images are rarely in a sufficiently good state to be mounted without careful attention. This may mean that a new copyright work has been created (but see paragraph 12). In addition, most websites probably qualify for protection as databases as they should meet the definition of a database (see paragraph 577). They are pretty poor websites if they do not! So extraction and reuse of substantial parts of it would be excluded. However, if there is no copyright in the original material then there is no infringement of the communication to the public right.

## 707 How do the copyright questions that arise in the electronic world compare with those in the paper world?

There are many copyright questions which arise in the electronic world to which the answers are exactly the same as in the more traditional paper-based world. However, some issues are peculiar to electronic materials and some of the answers that are quite clear in the paper world are not so obvious when we deal with electronic materials. The introduction of new legislation on databases makes many of the answers different if the work is considered a database.

# 12

# Other matters

## International treaties

**708  What importance does international copyright have?**
Technically there is no such thing as 'international copyright'.
Each country has its own copyright laws but most major countries belong to some or all of the three international conventions. Under these treaties and conventions each country protects
the works produced in other countries as if they had been produced within its own borders, although usually works are not
protected in a country for longer than they would be in the
country of origin. So if a work is produced in a country where
protection lasts for 50 years, but is imported into a country
where protection lasts for 70 years, then the work would still be
protected for only 50 years in that country.

**709  Which are these three major conventions?**
The Berne Copyright Convention, the Universal Copyright

Convention and the Trade-Related Intellectual Property (TRIPS) element of the World Trade Agreement. A fourth, the WIPO Copyright Treaty, was agreed in 1996.

**710    Are there any countries that do not belong to any of these conventions?**

Yes, but the number is decreasing all the time. Those that have not signed one or more treaties cannot benefit from the liberalization of trade planned under the World Trade Agreement so there is an incentive to reform or improve national copyright laws in most countries.

**711    If a country does not belong to one of these treaties does this mean that its publications can be copied?**

Perhaps. Although not all countries belong to one of the international treaties, one or two have signed bilateral agreements with the UK for mutual protection. It is best to check the latest SI (see Section 1).

**712    What is the importance of the Copyright Symbol ©?**

The idea of the © Symbol is to indicate the work is protected by copyright in the country of origin and had been registered for copyright protection. This is important under the Universal Copyright Convention as publications without the symbol are not regarded as protected. As the USA has now joined the Berne Convention, under which no formality is required for registering a copyright document, the symbol is chiefly important on publications from those countries that belong to the UCC but not to Berne. It also protects publications in those same UCC countries, so it is important for publishers to include it on their works even if it is not required in the country of origin, as it should protect them when exported to UCC countries. Lack of the symbol in most countries has no significance.

# Legal deposit

### 713   What is the connection between copyright deposit and copyright law?

None, nor has there been for many years. Copyright deposit is there to enable the designated libraries to build up collections of the publicly available material produced in the UK. The law was radically revised in 2003 under the Legal Deposit Act 2003, which includes enabling legislation to protect and manage copyright for electronic materials deposited with the designated libraries.

### 714   Why is it called copyright deposit?

Because it used to be a prerequisite for being able to claim copyright. But international conventions require that no formality is necessary before claiming copyright. Really, copyright deposit should now be called 'legal deposit'.

# Public Lending Right (PLR)

### 715   Is there a connection between PLR and copyright?

Yes. This was not true until the introduction of the lending and rental legislation but PLR and copyright are now firmly linked.

### 716   What is the connection between ISBNs, ISSNs and copyright?

Absolutely none. ISBNs, ISSNs and similar numbering systems are essentially tools of the bookselling and publishing industry, which have been hijacked by librarians as useful systems for cataloguing, identifying and locating. Their presence or absence from a document has no bearing on its copyright status.

### 717   There has been a lot of talk about a right called 'droit de suite'. What is it?

'Droit de suite' is a right given to the creator of an original work of art (painting, sculpture, and so on) so that each time the work is sold the creator receives a percentage of the increased price, if there is one. This means that a painter who starts off as unknown and sells paintings for a few pounds can benefit from any subsequent fame achieved.

**718 Does this have anything to do with libraries or archives?**
Only if they have, or plan to acquire, collections of original works of art.

**719 Has this right been introduced into the UK?**
No, not yet. It was agreed by the European Parliament early in 1997 but it may take up to ten years to become effective in the UK.

## Other legislation

**720 New human rights laws in the UK guarantee individuals the right of free speech. Can copyright be seen as infringing this human right?**
No, because the assertion of the right of free speech cannot be used to take away private property from someone else. As copyright is a property law, this means you can express yourself any legal way you wish but not use someone else's property to do it.

**721 How does copyright interact with data protection?**
Although most data covered by the Data Protection Act will be liable to database right, the rights conferred by the Data Protection Act do not change the rights of owners of database right at all.

**722 What about freedom of information laws?**
Again, rights of access to information do not change the rights of owners of the copyright in that information. Freedom does not mean it is delivered free of charge.

# 1

# List of useful addresses

**Authors' Licensing & Collecting Society (ALCS)**
Marlborough Court
14–18 Holborn
London EC1N 2LE
Tel: 020 7395 0600
Fax: 020 7395 0660
E-mail: alcs@alcs.co.uk
www.alcs.co.uk

**British Copyright Council**
29–33 Berners Street
London W1T 3AB
Tel: 01986 788122
Fax: 01986 788847
E-mail: secretary@britishcopyright.org.uk
www.britishcopyright.org.uk

**Christian Copyright Licensing International**
PO Box 1339
Eastbourne
East Sussex BN21 4YF
Tel: 01323 417711
Fax: 01323 417722
www.ccli.co.uk

**CILIP: the Chartered Institute of Library and Information Professionals**
7 Ridgmount Street
London WC1E 7AE
Tel: 020 7255 0500
Fax: 020 7255 0501
E-mail: info@cilip.org.uk
www.cilip.org.uk

**Copyright Licensing Agency**
90 Tottenham Court Road
London W1P 9HE
Tel: 020 7631 5555
Fax: 020 7631 5500
E-mail: cla@cla.co.uk
www.cla.co.uk

**Design and Artists Copyright Society**
Parchment House
13 Northburgh Street
London EC1V 0AH
Tel:  020 7336 8811
Fax: 020 7336 8822
www.dacs.co.uk

**Educational Recording Agency**
New Premier House
150 Southampton Row
London WC1B 5AL
Tel: 020 7837 6222
Fax: 020 7837 3750
E-mail: era@era.org.uk
www.era.org.uk

**HMSO Copyright Section**
St Clements
Colegate
Norwich NR3 1BQ
Tel: 01603 521000
Fax: 01603 723000
www.hmso.gov.uk

**Ministry of Defence**
Hydrographic Department
Finance Section
Ministry of Defence
Taunton
Somerset TA1 2DN.
Tel: 01823 337900

**Music Publishers' Association**
3rd Floor
Strandgate
20 York Buildings
London WC2N 6JU
Tel: 020 7839 7779
Fax: 020 7839 7776
E-mail: info@mpaonline.org.uk
www.mpaonline.org.uk

**Newspaper Licensing Agency**
Lonsdale Gate
Lonsdale Gardens
Tunbridge Wells
Kent TN1 1NL
Tel: 01892 525273
Fax: 01892 525275
E-mail: copy@nla.co.uk
www.nla.co.uk

**Ordnance Survey**
Copyright Branch
Romsey Road
Maybush
Southampton SO9 4DH
Tel: 01703 792706
Fax: 01703 792535
www.ordsvy.gov.uk

**Ordnance Survey Northern Ireland (OSNI)**
Colby House
Stranmillis Court
Malone Lower
Belfast BT9 5BJ
Tel: 028 9025 5755
Fax: 028 9025 5700
E-mail: osni@osni.gov.uk
www.osni.gov.uk

**Performing Right Society**
29–33 Berners Street
London W1T 3AB
Tel: 020 7580 5544
Fax: 020 7306 4455
www.prs.co.uk

## Phonographic Performance Ltd

1 Upper James Street
London W1F 9DE
Tel: 0207 534 1000
Fax: 0207 534 1111
www.ppluk.com

## Public Lending Right Office

Richard House
Sorbonne Close
Stockton-on-Tees TS17 6DA
Tel: 01642 604699
Fax: 01642 615641
www.plr.com.uk

# 2

# Further sources of information

Some useful books, journals and websites are listed below. The books must be viewed in the light of the dates on which they were published and will almost all need updating.

## Books

Armstrong, Chris and Bebbington, Lawrence W. (eds) (2003) *Staying Legal: a guide to issues and practice affecting the library, information and publishing sectors*, 2nd edn, London, Facet Publishing. ISBN 1 85604 438 6.

Cornish, Graham P. (2002) *Copyright in a Week*, 2nd edn, London, Hodder & Stoughton. ISBN 0 340 84944 4.

A very general introduction for users, owners and creators.

Cornish, Graham P. (2003) *Keep it Legal: copyright guidance for school library staff*, Swindon, School Library Association. ISBN 1 903446 21 X.

Flint, Michael F. (1997) *A User's Guide to Copyright*, 4th edn, London, Butterworths. ISBN 0 406 04608 5.

Garnett, Kevin et al. (1999) *Copinger and Skone-James on Copyright*, 14th

edn (2 vols), London, Sweet & Maxwell. ISBN 0 421 589 108.
The copyright bible.

Henry, Michael (1998) *Current Copyright Law*, London, Butterworths. ISBN 0 406 896208.
Gives the full text of the original Copyright Designs and Patents Act with all the amendments included in their correct place. This avoids the need to keep switching from one book to another.

Laddie, Hugh et al. (2000) *The Modern Law of Copyright and Designs*, 3rd edn (3 vols), London, Butterworths. ISBN 0 406 91004 9.

Norman, Sandy (2004) *Practical Copyright for Information Professionals: the CILIP handbook*, London, Facet Publishing. ISBN 1 85604 490 4.

Padfield, Tim (2004) *Copyright for Archivists and Users of Archives*, London, Facet Publishing. ISBN 1 85604 512 9.

Pedley, Paul (2000) *Copyright for Library and Information Services Professionals*, 2nd edn, London, Aslib/IMI. ISBN 0 85142 432 5.

Pedley, Paul (2003) *Essential Law for Information Professionals*, London, Facet Publishing. ISBN 1 85604 440 8.
Covers a wide range of legal issues of which copyright is just one.

Phillips. Jeremy (1999) *Butterworths Intellectual Property Law Handbook*, 4th edn, London, Butterworths. ISBN 0 406 92995 5.

Stokes, Simon (2001) *Art and Copyright*, Oxford, Hart Publishing. ISBN 1 84113 225 X.

Wall, Raymond A. (2000) *Copyright Made Easier*, 3rd edn, London, Aslib. ISBN 0 85142 447 3.

Wienand, Peter, Booy, Anna and Fry, Robin (2000) *A Guide to Copyright for Museums and Galleries*, London, Routledge. ISBN 0 415 21721 0.

## Periodicals

*Aslib Guide to Copyright* (1994) London, Aslib.
An ongoing loose-leaf publication.

*Copyright Bulletin*, Unesco, Paris.
Quarterly.

*Copyright World*, London, Intellectual Property Publishing.
Published six times a year.

*European Intellectual Property Review*, ESC Publishing, Oxford.
 Monthly.
*Industrial Property and Copyright*, World Intellectual Property Organ-
 ization, Geneva.
 Monthly.
*Managing Information*, London, Aslib.
 Has useful news and newsletter sections, available online to sub-
 scribers.

## Websites

www.alcs.co.uk
 The Authors' Licensing and Collecting Society website has links to
 all other licensing agencies in the UK.
www.bbc.co.uk/news
 Surprisingly useful for latest news on copyright, especially in the
 media.
www.cilip.org.uk/groups/laca/laca.html
 The website for the Libraries and Archives Copyright Alliance, which
 brings together most of the major players in the information provision industry to discuss copyright.
www.cla.co.uk
 The website for the Copyright Licensing Agency.
www.copyrightcircle.co.uk
 For information on courses and to put general copyright questions.
www.courtservice.gov.uk
 Gives official transcript of major cases. It is searchable by subject.
www.eblida.org
 Useful for European developments, especially relating to libraries.
www.hmso.gov.uk
 Latest information on use of Crown Copyright material.
www.intellectual-property.gov.uk
 A website maintained by the Patent Office to give information on a
 wide range of intellectual property issues. Copyright is well covered
 and there is a frequently asked questions page.

www.licensing-copyright.org

Useful for links to other licensing agencies. Focuses on school copy-right issues.

www.nla.co.uk

The website for the Newspaper Licensing Agency.

www.wipo.org

To keep up with international developments in the World Intellect-ual Property Organization.

# 3

# Commercial or non-commercial purpose?

Please note that the examples given below are *non-exclusive* and *do not constitute* legal advice. They are given for broad guidance only to library, information, archive and museum staff with the proviso that it is unwise for them to attempt to advise users (who should make up their own minds as to whether or not their copying is 'commercial' before proceeding). This is important as staff cannot be expected to offer legal advice to users and have no protection if they do so. These examples are based on some produced by Professor Charles Oppenheim of Loughborough University.

These might be considered to have a non-commercial purpose:

- work done by day-release students who are in employment but undertaking further education outside their place of work
- work done by lecturers entirely for their students
- articles for scholarly journals or papers for conferences unless a fee is expected
- work done for personal professional development

- work done exclusively for an NHS trust.

These might be considered to have a commercial purpose:

- company R&D
- market research
- information brokerage
- articles or papers where a fee is offered
- work done for spin-off companies owned by universities or similar
- work done for a private medical facility, including copying that is to be used partly for private work and partly for NHS work
- work done by students for an employer while on placement
- research done by students that it is known or expected will be used for commercial purposes
- work done by charities or non-commercial organizations to earn income even if it is then used to further the charity's aims
- work done by for-profit companies to earn money that is covenanted to a not-for-profit organization or charity
- training or professional development funded by an employer, which is linked to a commercial company's work or linked to carrying out a commercial activity.

The status is uncertain in these cases:

- work done by staff or students in academia sponsored by a commercial company but not necessarily for the benefit of that company
- work done for charities to raise funds
- work done to gain a qualification that will ensure a pay rise.

# 4

# Statutory declaration forms

## FORM A

## DECLARATION: COPY OF ARTICLE OR PART OF PUBLISHED WORK

To:

The Librarian of ........................................................................ Library

[Address of Library]

Please supply me with a copy of:

*the article in the periodical, the particulars of which are [                    ]

*the part of the published work, the particulars of which are [                    ]

required by me for the purposes of research or private study.

2.   I declare that:

(a)   I have not previously been supplied with a copy of the same material by you or any other librarian;

(b)   I will not use the copy except for research for a non-commercial purpose or private study and will not supply a copy of it to any other person; and

(c)   to the best of my knowledge no other person with whom I work or study has made or intends to make, at or about the same time as this request, a request for substantially the same material for substantially the same purpose.

3.   I understand that if the declaration is false in a material particular the copy supplied to me by you will be an infringing copy and that I shall be liable for infringement of copyright as if I had made the copy myself.


†Signature ...............................................

Date ...............................................

Name        ...............................................................

Address     .................................................................

              .................................................................

              .................................................................

*Delete whichever is inappropriate.

†This must be the personal signature of the person making the request. A stamped or typewritten signature, or the signature of an agent, is NOT acceptable.

# FORM B

# DECLARATION: COPY OF WHOLE OR PART OF UNPUBLISHED WORK

To:

The *Librarian/Archivist of ............................................................. *Library/Archive

[Address of Library/Archive]

Please supply me with a copy of:

the *whole/following part [particulars of part] of the [particulars of the unpublished work] required by me for the purposes of research or private study.

2.  I declare that:

(a)  I have not previously been supplied with a copy of the same material by you or any other librarian or archivist;

(b)  I will not use the copy except for research for a non-commercial purpose or private study and will not supply a copy of it to any other person; and

(c)  to the best of my knowledge the work had not been published before the document was deposited in your *library/ archive and the copyright owner has not prohibited copying of the work.

3.  I understand that if the declaration is false in a material particular the copy supplied to me by you will be an infringing copy and that I shall be liable for infringement of copyright as if I had made the copy myself.

†Signature .................................................

Date .................................................

Name      .................................................................

Address   .................................................................

          .................................................................

          .................................................................

---

*Delete whichever is inappropriate.

†This must be the personal signature of the person making the request. A stamped or typewritten signature, or the signature of an agent, is NOT acceptable.

# Index

**Note:** Reference numbers indicate paragraphs, unless specified otherwise.